CAMBODIA ANGKOR
A LASTING LEGACY

A view of it's Past and Present

by Pierre Odier

Dedicated to all the Children whose normal life in Cambodia has been interrupted and now are living at the Cambodian Landmine Museum in Siem Reap and to my grandchildren Nathan, Zachary, Cameron and Emerson.

www.limageodier.com

L'Image Odier Company
Publishing Since 1980

Copyright © 2010 by L'Image Odier Publishing Co. All right reserverd. Printed in China by Twin Age Ltd. No part of this publication may be reproduced, stored in a retrieval system, or transmitted, in any form or by any means. Electroni, mechanical, photocopying, or otherwise, without the prior written permission of the publisher, except in the case of brief passages quoted in connection with critical articles or reviews.

Library of Congress Catalog Card Number: 2010912704
Book Trade Distribution by L'Image Odier
1255 Hill Dr, Eagle Rock, CA 90041 - 1610
Hard Cover ISBN 978-0-9611632-9-7
Soft Cover ISBN 978-0-9611632-1-1

TABLE OF CONTENTS

Acknowledgments	6
Introduction	7
Foreword	9
History	11
Monuments	22
Culture	38
Conflicts	47
Traditional Dance	66
Music	87
Land mines	103
The Khmer Rouge	110
Cambodian Demining	127
Postscript	131
Bibliography	132

ACKNOWLEDGEMENTS

The creation of this book could not have been possible without the help of many individuals scattered in the USA and the word. Special gratitude to all the individuals in Cambodia who help identify the location of my old images dating back to the 1920. They all helped without understanding exactly what I was trying to accomplish. Your friendship, blind faith and trust you extended to me and my project was touching and deeply appreciated.

Very special thanks must go to the individual who accompanied me to all these remote difficult to reach sites in Angkor Wat. Bout Sokkhoeun was the person who guided me for the three years it took to locate all those lost ruins. Your loyalty for the three years and your relentless effort in finding individuals who could help in the identification process is what made this project a total success. To Mrs. Vong Metry, my deepest respect and thanks for allowing me the deep insight into your work preserving Cambodia's traditional art form: the dance.

In Cambodia we find some very special people who want to make Cambodia safe for its people and especially the children who are landmine victims. To all those children, Akira and his small staff at the landmine museum, who made me, feel so welcome into their world I extend my gratitude and dedicate this book to you.

The full page black and white images from the 1920 came to me over the years without the identity of its originator. I can assure you that every effort has been made to locate and acknowledge the source of the original material used in this book, which was a major task in itself.

I have tremendous gratitude for the people who helped me with the 21st century way of doing things. To Xun Chi who transformed all my pencil layouts and designs into intelligent, beautiful and techno correct format, I bow to you in respect and give you my profound gratitude. To Dan Kimber, my loyal editor who again took on the not so easy task of keeping my ramblings on task and balancing within a framework that responds to subject matter and the all over the place author. Dan you have most sincere gratitude for a job well so done.

Last but certainly not least a big thank you to the staff of Twin Age Limited Li Suk Woon. Suk Woon again did Twin Age Ltd proud by attending to my project. Thank you for again standing by my projects.

INTRODUCTION

In the mid-1980s, the award-winning movie "The Killing Fields" launched the Cambodian tragedy into the public consciousness. It deals with the genocide of nearly half the population of Cambodia at the hands of the Khmer Rouge which was the ruling Communist Party between 1975-1979.

Today, Cambodians are trying to put their past behind them and look to the future, yet their children know little and are not being told about the atrocities committed in their country. The genocidal policies of the Khmer Rouge not only obliterated lives, it also systematically erased historical records of the ancient traditions and rich cultural heritage of the Cambodian people.

The Khmer dynasty was one of the most powerful kingdoms in Southeast Asia. Its greatest legacy is Angkor, the site of the capital city during the empire's zenith. Angkor bears testimony to the Khmer empire's immense power and wealth, as well as the variety of belief systems that it incorporated over time. Modern researches by satellites have revealed Angkor to be the largest pre-industrial urban center in the world.

Cambodia is at once breathtakingly beautiful and unsightly taking in both the country and its people. It is easy to focus on the gloom and garbage that pervades this country of 10 million survivors and spawn of the Khmer Rouge genocide and its aftermath. The squalor and debasement in the slums where far too many are forced to live, from the grinding poverty of outlying rural areas crowded with beggars and one-legged/no-legged victims of this land riddled with unexploded land mines, one is overcome with the sense of utter hopelessness for this country's future.

I have tried to find words for what I have seen and for the people that I have encountered, but how does one describe the heaviness that lingers in a country that brutally murdered a quarter of its own population, its own people?

Most of you reading this will be doing so from a vantage point worlds away from the people and the culture described in this book. And from that safe distance where access to information has never been easier, where our global interconnectedness has never been so extensive, we can learn all about a troubled nation and a tragic people.

We can teach our children about man's inhumanity to man and set the record straight about who did what to whom, but the lesson should not end there.

The real lesson of Cambodia is found in the people who have survived the depravations of their past, who have been subjected to unspeakable atrocities, who have suffered inhumanity that most of us can only imagine—but whose will to survive, whose irrepressible spirit, whose pride in a heritage-even if confined to a small minority of dedicated people--all persist against all odds, and those are the true lessons of Cambodia.

Wood-Engraving Illustration by M.M.Ripley Estes & Lauriat, Boston, 1879

FORWARD

I was at an annual Pasadena Antique show and there under a table full of expensive Hispanic art was a box full of yellow old dog-eared envelopes used to protect photographic negatives. What immediately caught my eye was the word Siam on one envelope. That name told me that whatever was in the box was from before June 23, 1939, when that country became Thailand.

I wasted no time putting in an offer for the envelopes which was immediately accepted an I rushed home with approximately1000 four by five negatives in it. I could not determine who the photographer was but the pictures covered not only Siam but also Bali, China, Java, Viet Nam, Hong Kong, Nanking, Shanghai and Cambodia. I had stumbled upon an absolute archival treasure. From some of the dates on the envelopes I determined that all images where created in 1920.

Of all the negatives the ones that got my attention were from Cambodia. These images were absolutely fascinating and depicted the ruins at Angkor Wat. I immediately printed them up in my darkroom. The moment the images began to take shape in the developing tray I was hooked. I wanted to see more. I wanted to learn more about this mystical place on the other side of the world. So off I went to see for myself and create my own images.

In Cambodia I found a young man who was willing to help me find the exact locations of my old images. It took us eight days to locate the sites and for the most part we were able to position my camera in the same spot as the mystery photographer of 1920. What started as a curiosity turned into a bit of an obsession. I wanted to capture the changes that time and the elements and neglect had wrought on this grand monument by placing the old and new photos side by side.

What I also found in this place were people who have persevered in the face of long suffering but who are, at the same time, in danger of losing touch with a glorious past and a magnificent culture. In spite of an indifferent outer world to their enormous struggles, there persists a faint but discernable spark of commitment to preserve the threads that connect them to their ancestors and a proud heritage.

This book pays tribute to that commitment and the modest hope that that spark is never extinguished.

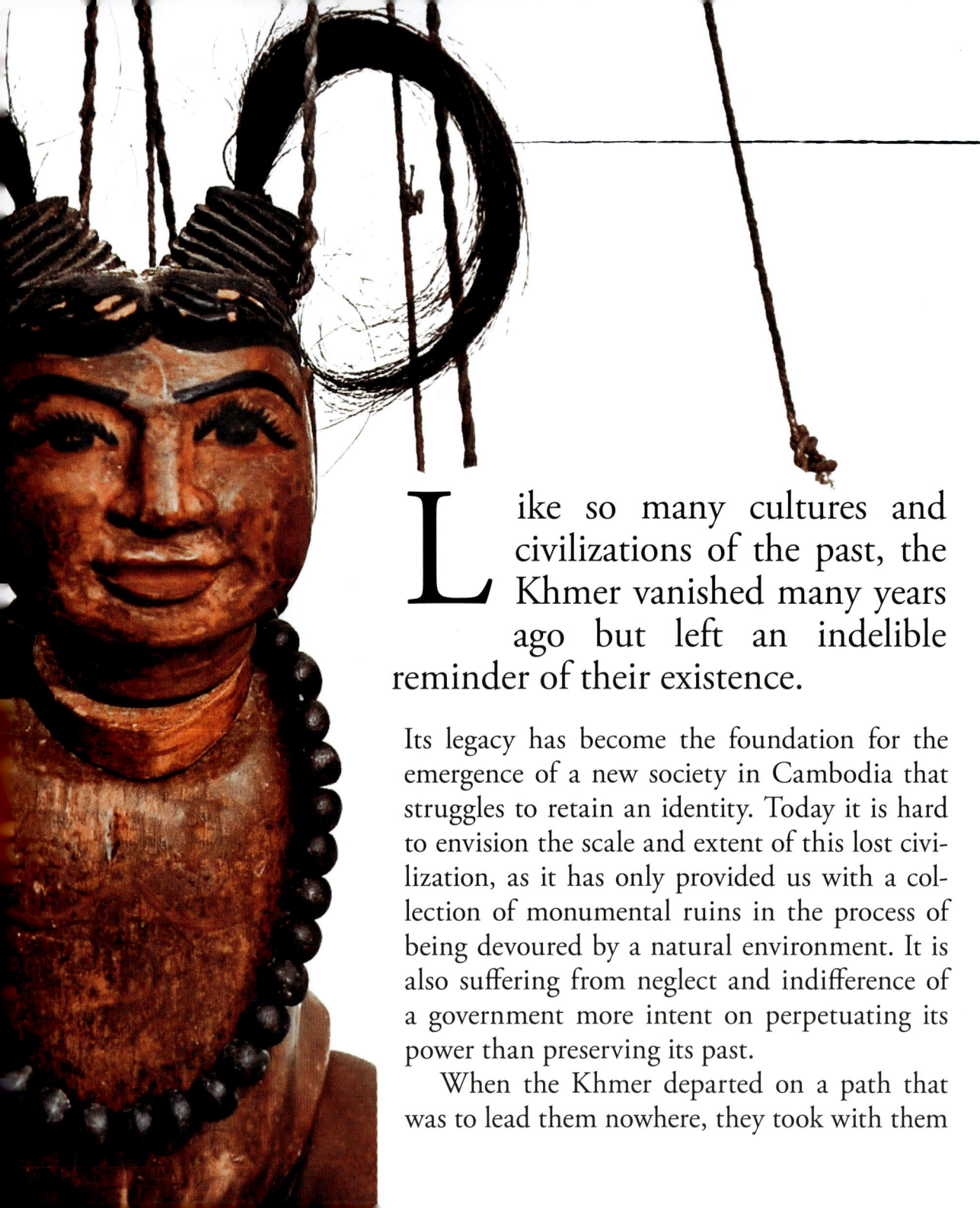

Like so many cultures and civilizations of the past, the Khmer vanished many years ago but left an indelible reminder of their existence.

Its legacy has become the foundation for the emergence of a new society in Cambodia that struggles to retain an identity. Today it is hard to envision the scale and extent of this lost civilization, as it has only provided us with a collection of monumental ruins in the process of being devoured by a natural environment. It is also suffering from neglect and indifference of a government more intent on perpetuating its power than preserving its past.

When the Khmer departed on a path that was to lead them nowhere, they took with them nothing more than the memory of their great culture. What must have been a painful realization, or perhaps it was a sense of foreboding that gave rise to the many legends relating to their lost culture and their explanation for its disappearance. These legends would offer them some hope of a possible rebirth of what is now an abandoned culture. According to a legend related in their oral history an explanation is offered as to their hope: "In the forest are the ruins of our cities, in the valleys near the rivers are the bones of our people. Our Kingdom is dust and ashes and desolation, one day our glory will return. Some day someone will come to restore our cities and make Angkor once more the marvel of the world".

Angkor is indeed one of the great marvels of the world. Considering the thousands of international tourists now wandering through these temple ruins each year, there is every chance that the fervent hope expressed in the legend of the Khmer will one day be realized.

This legend was being passed along well before westerners had discovered Angkor. When the natives did make contact with western white man, they told them of their long held beliefs of the curse that was upon their region. It was

HISTORY

a curse believed to be so powerful that any incursion into the forest would be doomed. They did state that some temples were occupied but that was only on special occasions and for religious purposes. The curse of the high Gods, they maintained, was on the forest and had been there for hundreds of years. They reasoned that if there was no curse these great cities surely wouldn't stand empty.

As late as 1920 the legend of a large emerald Buddha generated a good number of expeditions to search it out. There were many theories of what might have caused its disappearance, including theft by the Thais, destruction by the Khmer Rouge and the possibility that it had been moved overseas. This left many searchers without real motivation to mount a serious expedition for the legendary Emerald Buddha. The locals believed that all the vast treasures of gold, emeralds, rubies, golden fabric and all the treasures from the temples and palaces were all buried by the fleeing kings under the temples, some continuing five stories beneath the surface.

Today there is no creditable explanation as to what happened to all this wealth, but many would-be explorers persist in the hope that the

TOP: First Cambodian Stamp 1951, replacing Indo-China stamps
MIDDLE: Cambodian national Patch
BOTTOM LEFT: Angkor Wat temple 1920

1920   Ta Prohm Temple 1186 12th Century King Jayavarman VII

2006

Old Khmer man in Ta Prohm Temple

treasures do exist and that they might discover them. One must take into account the turbulent war-torn history of the region and its many occupations by ruthless regimes. The geographic isolation alone makes any serious attempts at excavation unlikely. Dense and continuously growing jungles guard the secrets well. With each passing year, the dream of solving this mystery grows more remote, especially considering that that region is completely under the control of a military regime that closely guards against foreign incursion.

Since the locals fear and respect the gods who placed the curse on the jungle none will venture into the dark mystery, not even with the temptation of finding vast treasures, which in all likelihood they would immediately lose to the government. Thus the entire region with all

Exploration Commission at Angkor Wat 1866

its secrets and deep mysteries will remain unexplored unless and until the western or eastern foreigner, not bound by beliefs in the curse, would venture into this region.

So far it is the French that have devoted the most time and resources to the region. They restored and studied continuously from the beginning of the 20th century until 1972, at which time they had to leave due to Cambodia's civil war.

Marcello de Ribadeneyra a Portuguese wrote the first account of Angkor in a western language in 1601: "We suppose that the founders of the Kingdome of Siam (today's Thailand) came from the great city which is situated in the middle of a desert in the Kingdome of Cambodia. There are the ruins of an ancient city which some say was built by Alexander the Great or the Romans. It's amazing that no one lives there now, it is only inhabited by ferocious animals and

TOP: Colonial officials at Angkor Wat 1920
BOTTOM LEFT: Tourist brochure for Angkor 1921
BOTTOM FAR LEFT: Travel rates to Angkor 1921

1920 The terrace of the Leper King 12th century (Bayon Style)

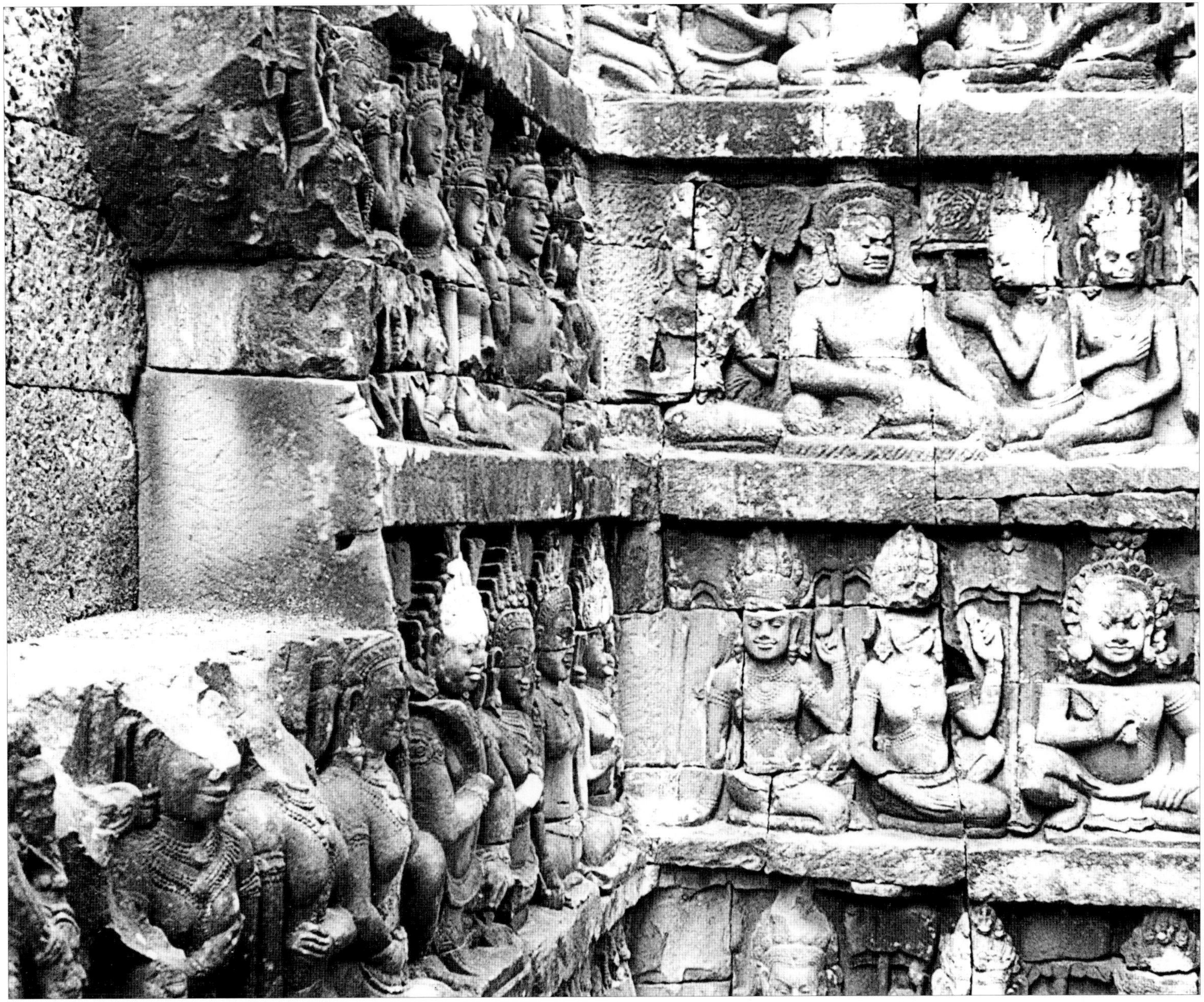

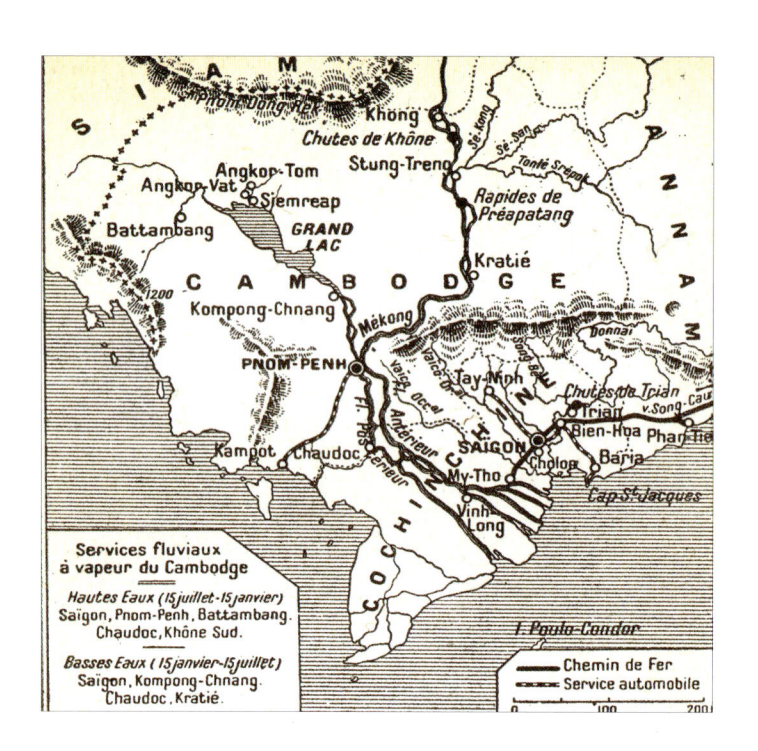

TOP LEFT: Old Cambodian map 1920
TOP RIGHT: King Suryavarman II (1115-1150) during an Audience on his throne

the local people say it was built by foreigners." Every written account by a western visitor reflects their absolute amazement and how awestricken they were upon viewing these well hidden monuments in the jungle. They are of such extraordinary construction that they defy description. Spanish missionaries in Cambodia in 1580 hoped to rehabilitate the ancient cities to become an out post for Christian missions. One report by a French missionary, Pere Chevrel, mentions that there was a very celebrated temple eight days from where he was and that it was known by his superiors in Rome. Possibly this man wanted to be assigned to that area in competition with other missionaries who were familiar with that region. An American Missionary living in Siam (Thailand) in the mid 19th century wrote a report on that region and may have had the same idea of moving to Angkor in order to establish a mission there. Competition for these remote regions was strong and even though much was written about Angkor, it mainly went unnoticed

TOP LEFT: Khmer homes near the temples 1918
TOP RIGHT: Book on Angkor published in 1924

in the west.

Only after a French Naturalist, Henry Mouhat, recorded in detail his observations was there a sudden interest in Angkor. He surveyed and measured the structures for inclusion in his simultaneous publications in London and Paris. He had only begun what looked to be a lifetime project when he suddenly died at the age of 35 from a tropical ailment. This abruptly brought to a halt what would have provided the world with the most comprehensive, detailed look at Angkor. Despite his untimely death, people from around the world wanted to see for themselves what this Mystery City was all about.

The most important publication came to the west in 1789 when the observations of the Chinese Diplomat Zhou Doaguan were translated into a western language. Zhou Doaguan visited Angkor in 1296 when the city was in full swing. His is the only known written detailed account of life in Angkor during its existence. He wrote detailed observations of the daily life

1920 Ta Prohm Temple 1186 12th Century

2007

MONUMENTS

TOP LEFT: Bas relief showing sinners taken to hell
TOP RIGHT: Tree roots taking over
BOTTOM: Bas relief Battle scene

after staying in the City of Angkor for eleven months. Since he was a member of the Chinese diplomatic mission he had a good opportunity to get close to the elite. His writings no doubt sparked great interest, though it was clear even then that life in Angkor was declining.

Being amongst these ruins today, deep in the lush forest, now standing in silent testimony of a glorious past, one is overwhelmed and challenged to imagine what this place must have been like during its cultural peak. Who else, beside the Khmer, stood here at the same spot? Over the many years there were invaders, occupiers, robbers, soldiers, wild beasts and nature itself all leaving their marks on this place. What remains today can best be described as the skeleton of a place stripped of all its flesh, lying lifeless but waiting to be revived.

What does remain here in the midst of these magnificent structures is the lingering spirit that reflects the creator of such a grandiose edifice. It invites the imagination to re-create images and reconstruct a past shrouded in mystery. The various bas reliefs and carvings left on many surfaces throughout the monuments offer mute evidence—elephants, battle scenes, ceremonies, processions, wild beasts and dancers—all visions

Zhou Doguang 1296 "Glories such as no man had ever seen before."

of a once thriving civilization. These images and fragments leave us with more questions than answers and until great effort is invested into the restoration and interpretation of what lay dormant for so long, the mystery will remain.

All descriptions of Angkor since Zhou Doaguan's only provide stark views of the ruins, much as they appear today.

Much time passed from the early discoveries of Angkor until an effort was made to preserve and study these astonishing monuments. It was not until the French took over the region in 1864 that real attention was given these vanishing monuments. Only after the laborious task of clearing this ever encroaching jungle could any study, much less reconstruction, take place. After the Ecole Francais d'Extreme-Orient was established in 1907, this region became the focus of some serious work to help understand and reclaim much of what was on the verge of disappearing. Sadly it was during that period that much of its fine statuary was archived and shipped off to France. Today much of what had been taken there can be viewed in many private collections as well as seen on display in several prominent museums throughout the world.

The sad irony of this is that some of these art

TOP: Bas relief army on the march
BOTTOM: Apsaras descending from heaven

1920 Ta Prohm Temple east walls 1186

2006

BELOW: 1921 Angkor tour guide
MIDDLE: Boy attending gas station 1920
RIGHT: Local transportation 1920

pieces are the best preserved today. During the period of French occupation, the entire region was off limits to the rest of the world. It was the French that conducted all the excavations and any work in regards to those monuments. Much of what the French were able to restore and preserve was destroyed after they left. Today one can see where the metal rods used to support some of the more imposing statues during restoration protrude. Even the help of concrete and steel did not prevent the looting and wanton destruction that took place over the years. Gunfire and land mines can be blamed for much of the visible destruction one can see today, but upon closer inspection it becomes very clear that much of what is damaged was done by power tools used by modern day looters. Power saws and jackhammers have been used to separate sculptures and figurines from their bases. It's clear that in order to loot the bigger objects teams had to be used, which leads to the conclusion that there was a lucrative market for the stolen artifacts.

LEFT: Bullet holes
RIGHT: Statue stolen leaving the base with its 1920 reinforcement rods

There is historical evidence that the destruction and looting of many monuments started in the 13th century, some of which were based on religious motivation. During this century the Hindu activists destroyed much of what represented Buddhism. This was done strictly in the name of religion and not for mercenary motives. The first large scale looting was done by the Thais during the 15th century and they managed to smuggle all their ill gotten gain into Thailand. After completing their raids on the Khmer capital, they took many of the collected treasures from various sources in the capital to sell back home. During later periods some monuments were ransacked, not for treasures but for materials to be used in their own constructions. Metal clamps used to hold stone structures together were a prime commodity. In the end, however, the advancing jungle prevented wholesale ransacking because of the difficulty in transporting the weighty objects of their desire.

It was during the 20th century that the

1920   Elephant Terrace 12th century King Yayavarman VII

2007

Even a cement reinforced statues was stolen off its base

world became very much aware of Angkor and its historical treasures, creating in turn a desire to own some of them. During that period the global art markets put out the word of a new source of wealth in the world, which renewed incentives for the thieves to go back to work in gathering up objects now much in demand in the west.

The most famous case of organized looting came at the hands of Andre Malraux, a French author and politician. Malraux and his accomplices explored through the deep jungles of Cambodia to find what they could loot. They happened upon Bonteay Srei, the first of the Angkor monuments to be rebuilt and the purest expression of Hindu architecture. They set up an extensive operation and were able to remove large parts of temples and ship them to Phnom

2009 preservation activities

Penh. Their misdeeds were discovered, all their loot was confiscated and Malraux himself was tried. In the aftermath of that it is interesting to note that Andre Malraux became Frances Minister of Culture in the Cabinet of Charles de Gaulle. In subsequent years the plundering became more and more organized and during the Vietnamese army's occupation a large quantity of art materials was stolen and sold cheaply in many different Bazaars. The larger and better pieces were smuggled to Thailand in order to fill the needs of the Bangkok dealers. From Bangkok the international market was much easier to reach than from any other location in Asia. Much was lost during that time period. Today the Royal Cambodian Government with help from UNESCO is taking measures to curb further marauding and help to preserve its

TOP LEFT: Head removed with chisels
TOP RIGHT: Heads removed with power tools
BOTTOM: Frieze of Apsara dancers 12th Century

1920   Banteay Kdei Temple 12th Century Buddhist

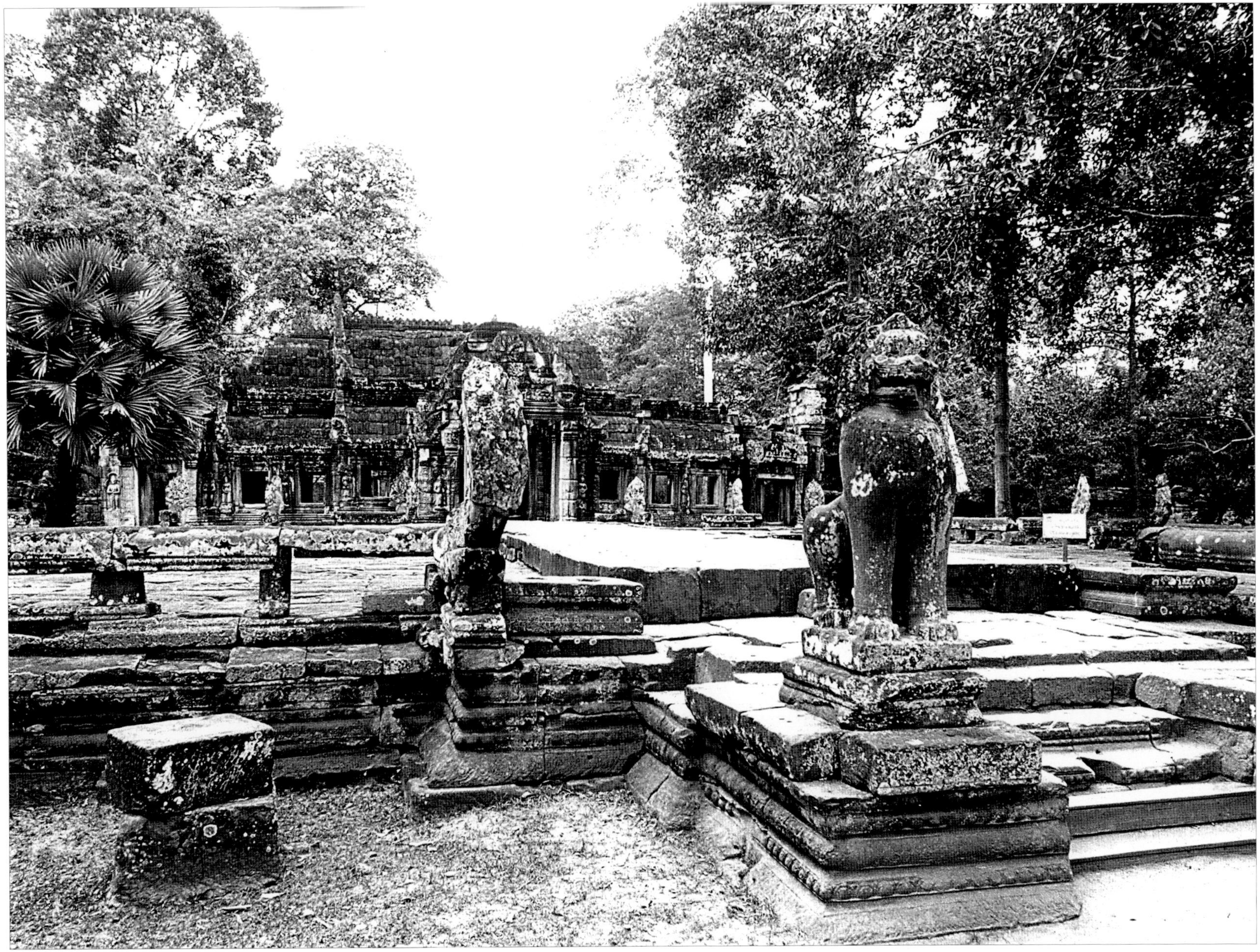

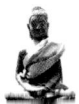

TOP LEFT: Produce vendor 1920
TOP RIGHT: Khmer Rouge Soldiers posing in front of Angkor Wat 1976

historical legacies. To prevent further thievery, a special police unit was formed, equipped with motorcycles and short wave radios linked directly to a central office. All the looted material is now being entered into a database for future reference with the hopes of locating stolen material.

What is left in situ today will help reconstruct the history of the Khmer. In order to do this the original inscriptions that have been discovered must be translated, since they provide the only correct link to their past history. This process was started during the French occupation but was interrupted by the Khmer Rouge period, creating more missing parts to this already difficult scientific job. These French translations do offer a glimpse into the post Khmer Rouge dynasties, and what remains is the painstaking task of reconstructing, piece by piece, past Kingdoms of a great civilization.

The question persists, "who were the Khmer"?, the answer is that there is very little information available on them. The earliest Khmer written records can be found in some of the monuments standing today, but only date back to the seventh century. Earlier information can be found in the journals of the early Chinese travelers through the regions of Southeast Asia. These texts are based solely on the observations of outsiders looking in on a newly discovered culture. A great deal of the information gathered was based on mythology, some of which survives up to the present day.

Based on these texts and what remains of physical evidence, in the first century AD a kingdom was established in the lowland valley of the Mekong. During that time period the Chinese were actively exploring these regions in order to expand their trade routes. Most of these explorations were expedited by the many waterways crisscrossing Cambodia which eventually brought them into the Mekong river and the Tonle Sap region. These regions contained well established settlements and were named by these travelers the kingdom of the Funan.

TOP LEFT: A Chinese grave yard 1935
TOP RIGHT: A Chinese head stone at Choeung Ek Killing Field 2008

1920 — Angkor Wat outer enclosure Library 12th Century

2007

CULTURE

TOP LEFT: Khmer Sanskrit on a temple column
TOP RIGHT: Peasants home near temple
BOTTOM: Khmer at the local market 1920

The Khmer Empire is the geographical and historical continuation of the small and prosperous Funan kingdom. Today some evidence of this original Funan kingdom can still be found in Viet Nam. The Funan kingdom must have been the result of early hunter and gatherers settling in this region who found there the necessary resources for their survival. There is evidence from that transition period of these early settlers' ability to cultivate rice. This allowed them to maintain a rice based existence and in turn gave them the needed tools to create an Empire based on trade and economic power in this region.

It is speculated that these early settled rice farmers probably spoke the ancestral Khmer language of Cambodia. Some traces of the Khmer language can still be heard spoken in Thailand today and other neighboring countries. It is estimated that during the Chinese Shang period the Khmer language was spoken in the entire region of today's Cambodia, but that there was no written language recorded that could be traced to any Austro Asiatic group. Without any written records, we can only trace the beginning of this culture through their settlements based on their rice cultivation. This provided the solid

Yin Natine 1927   "*The secrets of Ankor's existence may not have been known to the common people of Cambodia. But the kings always knew of it.*"

---

foundation for the Khmer empire to flourish starting with the overthrowing of the Funan empire in the sixth century. How this was accomplished is something of a mystery given the complete absence of written records during that period.

The first written record of the Khmer culture is in a form of Sanskrit now referred to as the classic language of the Khmer. The fact that it is a form of Sanskrit provides us with the evidence of the tremendous influence of India over the emerging Khmer culture. The main contribution to that entire region by India was their written language and their religion. This provided

TOP: Typical Khmer market 1920
BOTTOM: Khmer using the river to transport goods to the market In 1920

1931 Angkor Wat Temple recreated in Paris France

**ASSOCIATED PRESS PHOTO
PLEASE USE CREDIT**

FROM NEW YORK

INDO-CHINA IS BROUGHT TO FRANCE

FEB 27 1931

THE TEMPLE OF ANGKOR-WAT, INDO-CHINA, NEARING COMPLETION IN PARIS FOR THE INTERNATIONAL OVERSEAS EXPOSITION, WHICH WILL OPEN IN APRIL. THIS BUILDING WILL HOUSE THE INDO-CHINESE EXHIBITS. THE ARCHITECT SENT A REPRESENTATIVE TO ANGKOR, INDO-CHINA TO TAKE PICTURES AND MAKE MKR MEASUREMENTS, TO INSURE ACCURACY IN REPRODUCTION.

ASSOCIATED PRESS PHOTO
MET LIST KEY OUT 2/18/31 CA

2005

41

Jayavarman VII 1183
The leper king

"*He suffered more from his subjects diseases than from his own, for it is the people's pain that makes the pain of the kings and not their own.*"

BELOW: Monk in front of his home 1920
CENTER: Horse drawn Taxi 1920
RIGHT: Open air Restaurant 1920

all the various cultures in the region a way to express themselves. Neither the texts found in Cambodia nor the bas relief carved on the walls of Angkor shed much light on the culture of the daily life. They detail instead the various victories of the kings in the many wars. What can be gathered from the staues and carvings left behind is a wealth of information on their dress and weapons used in both ceremonies and battles. Additional insight into these people can be found in their incredible feats in architecture, temple layouts, hydraulics and elaborate systems of canals and dikes. These majestic projects attest to their ambitions and visions as well as their management of the natural resources of the area.

These visions were for the most part based on strict rules set out in religious doctrines well known in India. The Khmer temples all aspire to be the terrestrial images of their deity's heavenly abode. It would seem that ambition and vision alone would never be sufficient to create what is today regarded as one of the greatest achievement of ancient Asia. For any culture to be able to act upon visions of such a grand of scale there must be a means to implement it. What did these kings have that enabled them to materialize their visions? When the Khmer switched from hunting and gathering and settled into rice cultivation they found the means to create a wealth that would in turn fund the wars to acquire more land and the power to control the general population. They settled near rivers and lakes giving them access to the waters needed to support multiple crops a year. They learned to control the water supply by constructing dikes and flood control levies. Waterways, hydraulics systems, reservoirs were controlled by the Kings and the abundant grain supplies added to the kings' wealth and thus their power. They used their ability to control the water to create the lakes around their temples and palaces to symbolize the ocean surrounding the homes of the gods.

When King Indravarma stated that he would start digging five days after his inauguration it set into motion perhaps the greatest public work project in the country's history. The monarch's intention appeared in contemporary inscriptions and confirmed the construction of

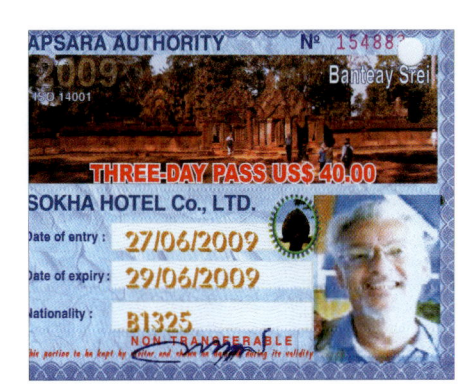

LEFT: Elephant used as transportation, as seen in a bas relief
CENTER: Pass to Angkor Wat used by the author
RIGHT: 12th Century sculptures face

1920   Eastern gate Naga Bridge, Preha Kahn 1191

2009

Lord Harris 1884 — *"How shall we describe these buildings which presents the only records of the great race that raised them?"*

the dike of the Baray of Roluos, the first reservoir in the Angkor region. This statement by a king gives us a small glimpse into the thinking of these leaders. They created these large public workforces with a commitment to build what today without a doubt are some of the grandest structures in the world. Yet the temples we see today provide us with only a sketchy idea of the total number of structures which can be attributed to the many visions of these Khmer Kings of Cambodia.

What we see today is a mixture of architectural styles dating back to the reigns of the various kings that ruled the Khmer empire. It is very evident that these builders were guided by a strong religious framework. There is no other place on Earth where architecture and sculpture are so perfectly blended. The early traders from

TOP: Grenade damage to building
BOTTOM: Frieze in a stat of natural erosion

CONFLICTS

India brought Hinduism and Buddhism to the newly emerging empire. The Khmer did not abandon their indigenous deities but worshiped them with less complete rituals than those from India. The imported religions from India combined with the ancient indigenous practices of the Khmer to create the unique Khmer vision which is evident in all the temples that were erected to provide a home for the various deities. The mixing of the statues of different styles and periods created a unique setting for the worshipers, reminding them of all the different religions now part of their culture.

From the beginning of the Khmer culture in 790 to 1327 we find many temples scattered throughout Cambodia, each addressing a different deity, but the Khmer national spirit was made captive in the stones we find in Angkor today.

Mines affect almost every aspect of life in countries emerging from conflict:
They reduce agricultural productivity, prevent refugees to return, hinder reconstruction, make roads impassable, cause large numbers of casualties and perpetuate the fear and anxiety caused by war.

TOP LEFT: Column with machine gun holes
TOP RIGHT: A bullet hole from a handgun, bullet still in place
BOTTOM: Police guards at the market 1920

1920

Srah Srang landing of Royal swimming pool 10th -11th Century
King Rajendravarman II (10th century) and King Jayavarman (11th Cetury)

2008

49

Today's craftsman restoring and creating new sculptures for some of the temple

Stone structures are what have survived over the centuries. Stone is what was used for the temples and wood was used for all the other dwellings. Wood is much easier to work with and less costly, which explains why wood was used for the cities around the temples. But wood cannot withstand the ravages of time or of environmental encroachment or of fire. This is the primary cause for the disappearance of all the surrounding cities and an insight into the daily life of the Khmer people. Wood was used also in small pavilions and in some beams in the temples and in the palaces of the rulers. Today there survives only a few foundations with limited information as to their intended purpose.

That the occupied area around the temples was vast can be seen in tracing some of the streets laid out in grid patterns during the empire time period. Some of these roads are still being used today. The dense forests of today are surely obscuring the actual size of these ancient cities. So again, we are left with only the accounts of the

NEWS

Cambodia Oct 27 2008 Two Cambodia soldiers were killed Oct. 15 when Thai and Cambodian troops exchanged fire at a border spot occupied by a disputed ancient temple. Today Cambodian soldiers patrolled the grounds of the Preah Vihear temple. As the Camboidan soldiers guard the temple, it also serves as a playground for Children.

LEFT: Preah Vihear Temple with lone monk 2010
CENTER: Soldier guarding Preah Vihear Temple
RIGHT: Soldier walking his guard bear

early Chinese texts to give us any kind of an idea as to life in cities around these temples.

The building materials used were few, but were used with great effect both in structural considerations and visual appearance. The first material used in the early structures were bricks. These bricks where hardened with a vegetable compound and did not particularly lend themselves to elaborate carving. So the earliest structures were much less ornate than the later ones that used stone materials. Sandstone would ultimately became the material of choice for these original builders of Angkor. Their counterparts in Europe were using the same materials in the building of their cathedrals.

For Angkor the source for the needed sandstone was the Kulen Mountains. These stones weighing up to four tones were transported via barges down the canals. On land they would transport them by wagons to the needed workplace. The holes that can be seen in some of these stones today were made to help handle

1920   Entrance of long causeway to the temple of Angkor Wat

2007

TOP LEFT: 1920 pottery and basket vendor at the market
TOP RIGHT: 1881 graffiti in a lion statue by R.H.
BOTTOM: Modern sculpture working on a Elephant sculpture

them with wood poles and ropes. Some of these upright monoliths where held together with iron anchors, clamp joints and braces. These metal clamps were a real treasure for the modern day scavenger who extracted the metals and then took them to the market to sell, causing some of the monuments to collapse. During the modern wars soldiers would take this material to use in their military campaigns. Some of the entry arches were created by staking the stone projecting out over the edge of the previous stone until they would meet at the top. Gravity would press them against each other keeping them from collapsing under their own weight.

Sandstone has a great advantage for the artist, soft enough that it can be carved without too much difficulty giving the artist-sculptor the means to create the wonderful decoration that covers all the surfaces of these temples. That is what remains for us to marvel at today and should continue to do so for centuries to come. This was their way of portraying their deities and decorative designs. The most common effect used by the Khmer builders was that of decreasing the height and width of the roof of the Pasat (pyramid temple), pyramid terrace and steps on the stairways. This makes the building appear taller than they actually were. This unique process is called stereo metric which is taught to all aspiring architects today.

The length of the unstable history of Cambodia in part is responsible for much of the missing evidence of this great culture. We do find small fragments of paint on some structures leading to a reasonable assumption that the surfaces of these temples were at one time covered with paint. When ground was broken for the construction of a new temple, there was always an elaborate ceremony. At that time an elaborate offering was made with precious stones and gold that would be placed under the

TOP: 1920 outdoor restaurant

BOTTOM LEFT: Higher class restaurant notice table and server

BOTTOM RIGHT: Smoking (opium) pipes for the tourist trade

1920   Causeway entrance to Angkor Wat

2008

Lord Curzon   "*Angkor Wat is the most remarkable collection of ruins in the world*"

BELOW: Strap preventing an entryway from collapsing
CENTER: Deteriorating sand stone carving
RIGHT: Large carved stone blocks missing from sculpture Monumental face

foundation of the inner shrine. These offerings were placed in a square flagstone marked with letters and covered with a lid. Thieves armed with that knowledge went after these treasures and naturally destroyed much of the structure in ransacking temples in search of these offerings. This obscured the original architecture, never to be recreated, now lost forever.

The remaining ruins do provide us with some insight as to what must have been a vivid and flourishing culture which has left an indelible imprint on Cambodia's history and on its people. These remaining monuments provide us with an overwhelming sense of grandeur and at the same time, a sense of personal insignificance.

A vivid illustration of this unique culture can be seen in the figurative carvings found in all of the major structures. An astounding variety of figures each provides a different version of dress, hairstyle and expression. Much of the delicate details on these meticulous carvings are slowly eroding. On certain figures one can see only faint traces of tiaras, necklaces and details of the folds in the garments. In viewing these carvings the inventiveness and attention to details is still very apparent.

Today the race is on against this rapid and relentless erosion of the past. In a recent article in a daily publication the headline read, "Microbes eating away at pieces of history". In this article written by the noted journalist, Bina Venkatarman, he writes, "At Angkor Wat, the dancers feet are crumbling". This observation is disturbing on two fronts. The presence of a bacteria, gloeocapas, is the natural enemy of stone. It stains the rock carvings black and retains water that creates a daily expansion and contraction cycle that leads to an actual cracking of the stone, breaking away the carved details. On the second front is the permanent loss of cultural details that might shed light on Khmer views of themselves and their connection to the rest

FAR LEFT: Stone being affected by natural fungus
CENTER: Far advanced stone fungus
RIGHT: Roots slowly separating stone monuments
BOTTOM: Water damaged Apsara carvings held together by wires

1920 View into Temple hallway in Banteay Kdei

2009

of the universe. With no written language these details are of paramount importance in attempting to recreate this lost culture.

These crumbling carved figures, though silent witnesses in stone, are the remaining threads of preservation of the spirit of this mighty lost empire. All the details carved in stone document the type of Cambodian mythology that prevailed during the different time periods.

Today we know that these Khmer dances predate Khmer civilization. Their roots can be traced to India where they were firmly established in all of their enduring traditions. These traditional dances are what are handed down until this day. They are the Apsaras of Cambodia, the celestial dancers, who from the start never changed the classic dances taught to them by the masters. Everything stayed the same, the

LEFT: In the shadow of Apsara dancers
TOP: A bullet stuck in the Sculpture

"When I saw the girls dance I thought they came from paradise"   *Vong Metry*

---

costumes the stories and all the classic movements of body and hands. It is in the sculptures of the different time periods that we can observe the same consistency in all the details frozen in time We can recognize the dedication in the teaching of this classic traditional art form in order to stay so consistent over such a long time period. The carvers captured the essence of these dancers in stone but the teaching had to come from individuals that mastered over time the intricate details of this ancient art form. These traditional skills came to the dancers through a long vigorous training under the committed guides of these master dance teachers. Without those teachers this traditional art form would have vanished or at best changed into a new art form. These teachers had the responsibility of keeping the spirit and soul of Cambodia alive.

TOP LEFT: Bas Relief Apsara Dancers in the Hall of Dancers
TOP RIGHT: Apsaras with elaborate head dress
BOTTOM: Decorative pattern

1920 Leper King Terrace

2008

TRADITIONAL DANCE

Dance groups formed in probably every village and were taught by former royal dancers. The kings had large permanent dance groups at their palace and every girl dancer aspired to be included in such a royal dance group. Some girls were good enough to join an itinerant group providing them the opportunity to travel from village to village. They performed as long as they were enthusiastically received. For some girls the time spent with these itinerant groups gave them all the exposure and training needed to become court dancers. The royal court had its own students from within the royal dance troupe and it was the hope of every village girl to be recommended to the royal troupe. For a girl dancing became an avenue of escape from her ignominious village life. As a traditional dancer she became the sole preserver of the spirit of an

TOP: Dancers praying before a performance
BOTTOM LEFT: Bas Relief of dancers bringing offerings to Gods before there performance
BOTTOM RIGHT: Hand position meaning Fruit

ancient mighty empire. This idea is reflected in most all the temples in bas relief and murals. The finest examples can be found on the walls of Angkor . The representation of these celestial dancing girls in the temples gives us a clear view into the Cambodian mythology dating back to the ancient Khmer culture. In some inscriptions we can read that the king of Angkor had 615 royal dancers at his royal court. The most exact and consistent link between the past and the present were the Royal Ballet dancers. August Rodin in 1906 after seeing a performance of the Royal Ballet said, "These Cambodian women have given us everything antiquity could hold. It's impossible to see human nature reach such perfection. There is only this and the Greeks".

Dancing, the sole and spirit of the Khmer culture almost came to its end during the

TOP: Apsara in a formal position 2005
BOTTOM LEFT: Childs drawing of a dancer
BOTTOM RIGHT: Apsara dancers in a 12th Century Frieze

67

1920　View towards Angkor Wat from parking area

2008

Khmer Rouge ruling period. Pol Pot made every effort to extinguish the Royal Ballet. Teachers were systematically executed, instruments where smashed, costumes and books burned and all the musicians, artist and dancers were killed. Fortunately for Cambodia a handful of teachers fled to other countries or were able to hide during that time period. Today some of these survivors are attempting to teach the old traditional dancing to a new generation.

The stories of these few surviving teachers are incredible and worthy of preservation. But what is more enduring is how today they are the most important link to the past. As all the arts were systematically being destroyed by Pol Pot, what remained was locked in the minds of the few who managed to escape death. The surviving members of the Royal Ballet who ended up in refuge camps in Thailand made a sacred vow to honor their traditions by teaching the young their dances. In those dances are ancient rhythms and subtle movements

Different style of Apsaras in various location in Angkor Wat

TOP LEFT: Young student training on traditional old Instruments
TOP RIGHT: A grandmother helping young dancer with her costume

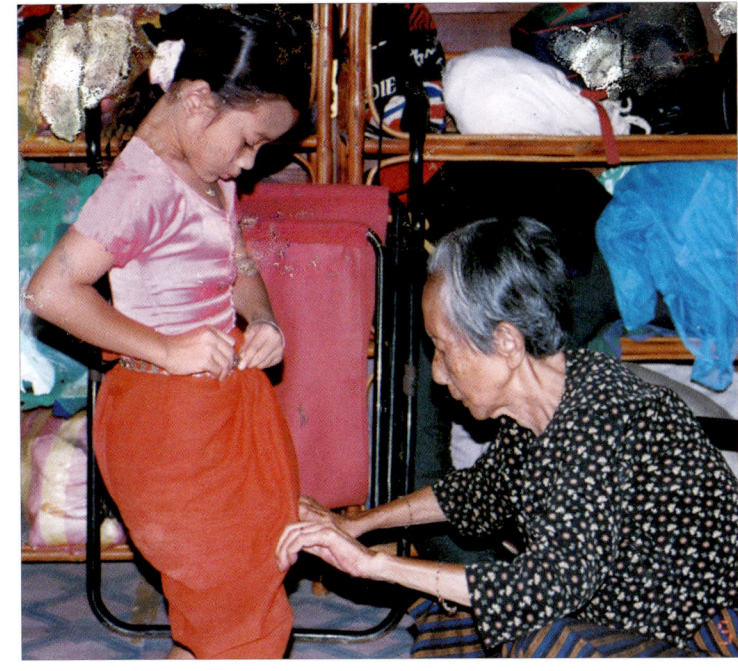

that tell a story of a proud people.

In the camps this helped morale and gave a focus to the children who might have languished in their confinement.

During the Royal times the children that were in the Royal Ballet group were from all parts of the country and represented all segments of society. This mixture of Cambodian children involved with the dancing established dance as part of the court life in which members of the royal family participated. This art form of royal Cambodian classical dancing has been associated with the royal court for thousand of years. It is a form of expression that dates from antiquity and has been handed down by the teaching of generation after generation. It survives not by written instructions, but by the knowledge of the teachers who pass it along to the young.

To think that this long-standing tradition of continuing the spirit and soul of a culture almost vanished overnight in the 1970s brings to mind the enormity and tragic effect of a ruling clique

1920 Preah Khan Temple 12th Century King Jayavarman VII

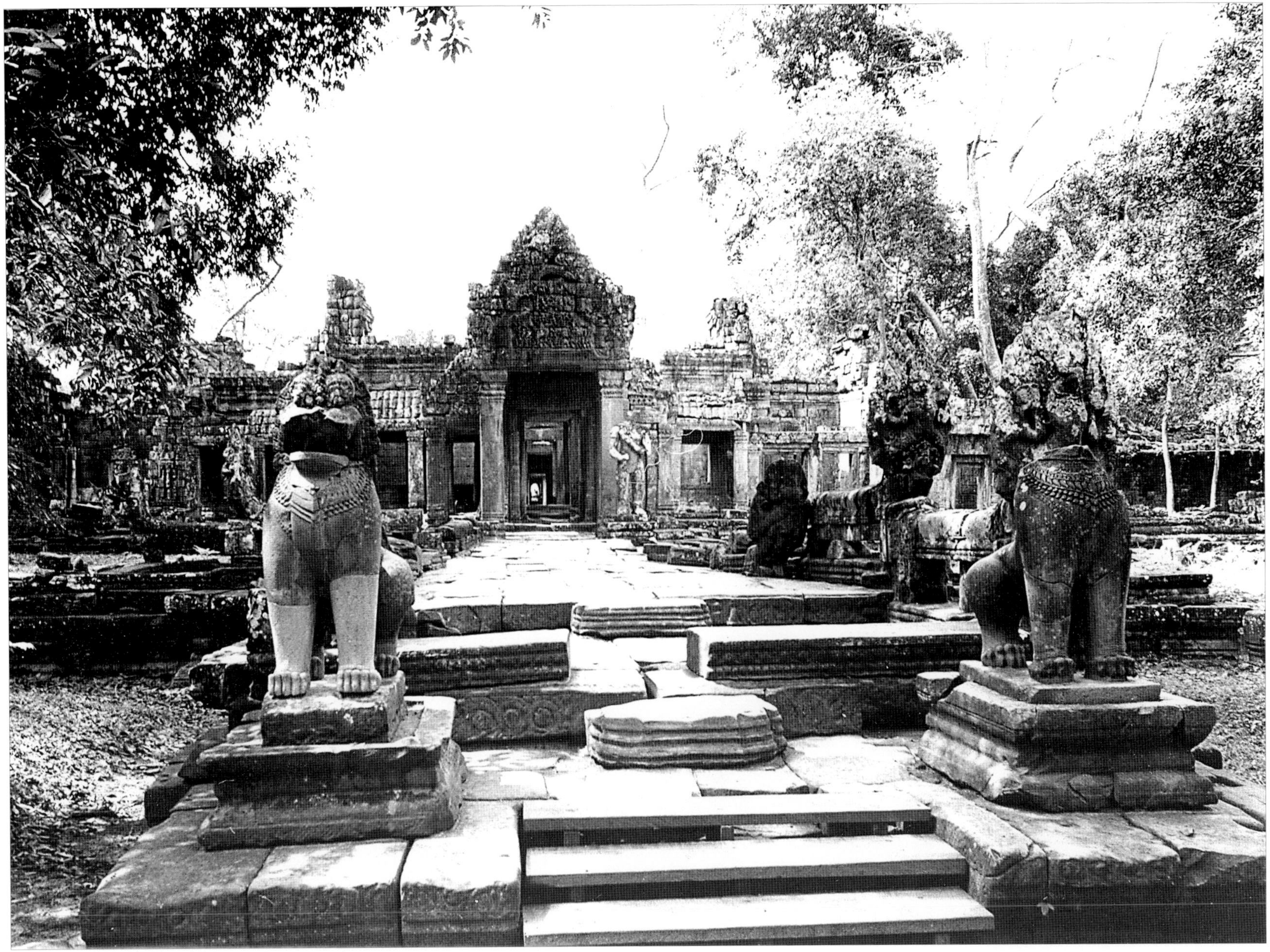

TOP LEFT AND RIGHT: Young dance students of Mrs. Vong Metry during practice
BOTTOM: Mrs. Vong Metry with here students 2008

that seized total power. Their brutal suppressions and cruel disregard for a great culture are now documented, but what is not well documented are the faint stirrings of a dedicated handful of people determined to hold on to a culture and a way of life in danger of disappearing altogether.

Today's teaching and training of Cambodians in the traditional classical dance form is a heroic attempt by a small but dedicated group of people intent on rescuing the very soul of a country. One such person is Mrs. Vong Metry who, with artists from the Royal University of Arts in Phnom Penh, formed the Apsara Arts Association in October of 1998. Before the students go to the Royal University of Fine Arts, where they train for nine years before becoming professional dancers, they attend Mrs. Vong Metry's school. Every day these students must go through a series of basic exercises which includes the bending of hands, fingers, wrists, elbows, waists and toes, to achieve full control of all that's needed to perform in the classical Cambodian dance routines.

The difficulty in finding or training teachers to help with this immense task is constantly on the mind of Mrs. Vong Metry as she attempts to further the arts of Cambodia. She works to see

Cambodian arts and culture become more valued and popular in today's Cambodia, as it once was. This is made all the more difficult because of the basic change in students' attitudes. The youth in Cambodia today have very little interest in the past and a correspondingly high interest in modern culture, most of it imported from the West. Videos, I Pods, cell phones and all the modern technology imports have captivated and preoccupied young people leaving little time and less inclination to keep ancient traditions alive.

It's difficult to calculate the sense of loss experienced by the artists at the Khmer Rouge.

TOP ROW: Mrs. Vong Metry giving individual guidance
BOTTOM LEFT: Dance puppet in the market place
BOTTOM RIGHT: Dance group in respectful bow for the audience

1920 Bayon Temple (1181) east gate

2008

LEFT: Dancers waiting to preform 1932
MIDDLE AND RIGHT: Dancers on Temple walls

We cannot ask the artists and historians for most have vanished and what is left behind is fragmented and covered in the silence of pain. Mrs. Vong Metry expresses what was on her mind during the days when she feared for her life. She said that she made a promise to herself that if she survived she would start a dance school and teach a new generation about the culture of Cambodia. As soon as the regime of Pol Pot's Khmer Rouge collapsed, she started the search for any dance teachers that might have survived the massive purges carried out by the Communist regime. The search became an almost impossible task since Cambodia was left with no infrastructure, no contact between villages and families from each village were scattered all around the country. In her search, Mrs. Metry could only locate two former dance teachers in the entire country.

She writes, "After the collapse of the regime and upon locating two teachers we immediately formed a dance group in Phnom Penh.

The first task was to create a dance; we did and called the dance, A Boat Of Cambodia Outside Cambodia".

"The only references I had were fragmented memories, so I asked the two other teachers to share and recreate the knowledge of a dance from our memory, and from that collaboration, we made up this dance." All the information in regards to the costumes and jewelry was gathered from the sculptures and bas relief on the walls of Angkor Wat. The re-creation based on what was seen in the temples is accurate except for the absence of color, so that information had to come from memory and remaining fragments scattered throughout the world. France has collected some material and is probably the largest archival depository of Cambodian art.

Mrs. Vong Metry's small dance and music school serves poor families and orphanages for many children throughout Cambodia students

Old Photographic images of Royal dancers

1920   Terrace of the Leper King Bayon style

2009

are instructed in subjects other than dance to acquire knowledge and skills that are best for the nation. Many students come to the dance school after attending their regular day school and, despite the fact that the great majority come from the poorest families, these children understand that they are participating in a noble effort to keep their Cambodian heritage alive. When they are taken on field trips to the temples to look at the carvings, they are better able to connect the past with the present and, hopefully, plant the seeds for the future as well. A valuable connection is established and hopefully will encourage these students to stay true to their heritage. The spirit in the stones at Angkor Wat is again coming to life, thanks to these dedicated and committed teachers.

One reality facing all of Cambodia's

TOP: Carving of Apsara dancers at Angkor Wat

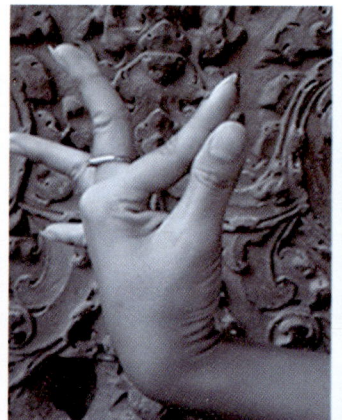

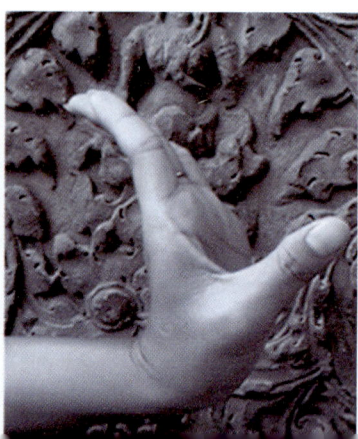

BOTTOM: Important traditional hand position of the dancers

educational institutions and the precious few dedicated teachers today is replacing what was obliterated back in the 70s. Many professionals in all fields were killed leaving a great intellectual void, not to mention the thousands of priceless artifacts that were destroyed. At a dance school in Phnom Penh that used to have thousands of students per year, only thirty attend today. The vice dean Nola Him states;" Because the funding so miniscule in this field, it is a struggle to get the students interested in traditional dance. Some of the original dance schools were sold to private companies and then were moved far from the city. With transportation presenting a problem it made it very difficult for a student to attend on a regular basis. The professionals are far and few between and are getting old. The younger ones are getting fewer and fewer every year".

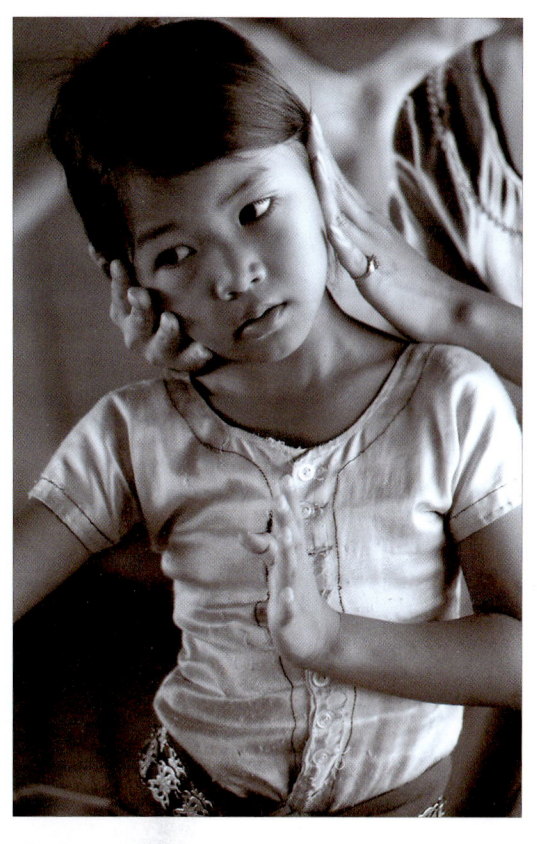

TOP LEFT: Dancers practice difficult hand position **TOP RIGHT:** Proper head positioning being practiced **BOTTOM:** Hand positions

1920 Bayon Temple 1180 12th Century with wild elephants

2009

"My ultimate dream is to be part of preserving the real Cambodia culture"   *Vong Metry*

When asked why dance is so important to Cambodia, the answer comes fast and without hesitation. "Dancing is so important to Cambodia's history because it reveals unique aspects of Cambodians as a people. It tells the world about our culture, beliefs and traditions of our grandfathers and its relationship to our history today".

In a tone of frustration she added," I teach dance from the bottom of my heart, but I am too old. I can't see well and am always sick. I just want the world to help save Cambodia's traditional dance.

These words and heartfelt sentiments spring to life when one is standing face to face with the mute stone carvings of the dancers in the walls

TOP: Indo Chine stamp with Apsara Celestial Dancer 1931
LEFT: Mrs. Vong Metry posing student in final position

MUSIC

of these temples. Their motions and carefully choreographed movements are frozen in time in silent testimony to a time and to a people forgotten by a nation and ignored by an outer world. These single dancers in their eloquent poses, carved by skilled artists, moves one to imagine what it must have been like to witness the full ensemble in harmonious motion depicting the elements of their long-standing mythology.

The imagination is helped along by the soft sound of instruments wafting in from the forest surrounding these carved dancers. It's a sound that seems to originate from the stone dancers themselves, but in fact this music is produced by a live musician just outside the main entrance to this temple. These are not just ordinary musicians gathered in small ensembles; they are victims of the ever present feared landmine presence in

TOP: Blind musicians playing old traditional instruments at the temple entrance
BOTTOM LEFT AND RIGHT: Abandoned streets in 1975

1975   Siem Reap street after Khmer Rouge evacuation order

2008

TOP: Landmine warning singe
RIGHT: Painting of landmine victims

Cambodia. These artists create a mood and a certain color to carvings frozen in stone brought to life by the rhythms coming from the forest. The sounds are precise and unique, unlike anything heard in today's contemporary music. The connection between these stone dancers and the music is an intimate bond and one that cries out to be revived—for historical accuracy and cultural pride and for the glorious preservation of a truly unique musical expression.

This music is created by individuals who have gathered in small ensembles throughout the country hoping to earn sufficient money to feed themselves and their families. Virtually all of these musicians are landmine victims who have suffered from one form of dismemberment or another. Employment for those individuals in Cambodia is next to impossible with only a small percentage of amputees finding work. Muscle power means work and it ultimately means survival. Families with an amputee receive less land to farm, because the land is divided based on the number of active adults in that family Physical impairment, regardless of how it came to be, consigns countless thousands of human souls to live a 'broken' life.

This is a country that has endured twenty years of famine, foreign occupation, civil war and genocide. The teaching of Buddhism in Cambodia emphasizes inner and outer "wholeness", thus preventing any boy or man who suffered from a landmine explosion from joining the ranks of the monks. This reality is especially hard on the children who became victims, for they now realize that there is no future for them in this society. To make matters worse, in many cases families abandon children at the hospital leaving them to fend for themselves. These children are now doubly impaired by their orphaned status. Many resort to begging, or worse, lives of crime.

A very few of these children find refuge in the few orphanages that will teach them a skill and a possibly a means to earn a living. Most

TOP LEFT: Girl placing flower on a young boys ear

TOP RIGHT: Flower placed on temple steps

1920   Pre Rup AD 961 view from the east stairway

2009

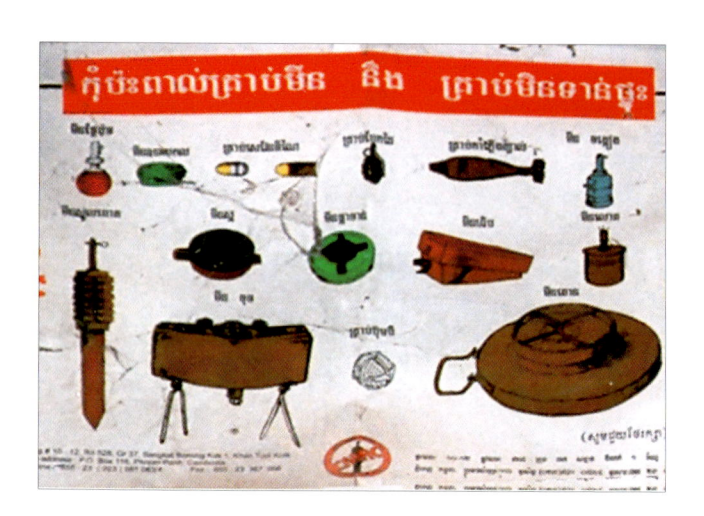

TOP LEFT: Landmine identification poster
TOP RIGHT: Childs painting of Angkor Wat
BOTTOM: Card written to a tourist by a child vender

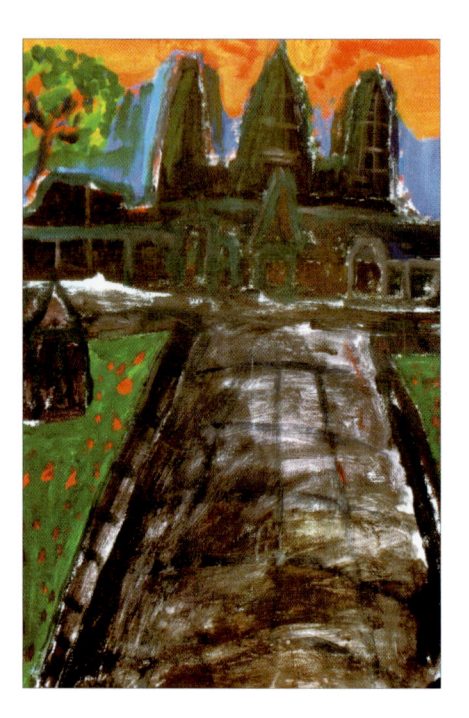

victims have to fend for themselves with very little help from their government and society.

Today the land mine problem is regarded as the major health hazard right along with malaria and tuberculoses. These landmines further impoverish the nation by limiting the amount of land distributed for farming.

Worst of all is the fact that there are no maps to show the location of the mines. If they were laid by the Khmer and if the person who laid the mines is still living, there is only a slim chance of locating bomb sites. It is only after an explosion that a field gets identified, which means most likely at the expense of life. In many villages the locals have declared questionable areas off limits out of fear of becoming victims. Countless animals and small children have ventured into these areas and thus become victims, regardless of the standing warnings by the elders. Many mines have been placed in strategic areas to discourage enemy soldiers and civilians from entering these areas to gain protection and cover. The temples can provide good cover for soldiers and are sought after as strategic positions from which to attack and, if necessary, to defend. That explains why so many mines were placed in those contentious areas. Those who suffered

94

the most from that practice were the local farming and herding communities. Today many mines remain, hidden in the ground and waiting to inflict the cruelest kind of injury. Dense overgrowth and natural vegetation have all but obscured original structures. Animals from time to time manage to crawl into that growth and detonate mines. In general, farmers try to build restraining fences but that doesn't prevent the occasional loss of an animal, or worse of a child exploring the fields.

These hidden land mines are very expensive to clear and therefore fall low on the priority list. The land that is cleared by the government is only to allow the building of roads and other infrastructure. The area left and right of the road doesn't get cleared, creating problems for man and beast who are unlucky enough to have their footsteps detonated. If these stretches of land could be cleared of mines, they would be distributed to farmers to cultivate.

It turns out that for some companies this clearing operation is a very lucrative and competitive business venture. In order for a company to do the de-mining business in Cambodia, it must first have the proper government approval and therein lie open opportunities for graft and

TOP: Landmine victims band

BOTTOM: Landmine victims selling their CD's

1920 Pre Rup AD 961 East Stairway

2009

Children of all ages selling items to tourists

payoffs. As it turns out, there is big money in land mine removal for the companies that do it, but absolutely no compensation is offered for the victims of land mine explosions.

These victims, that include the very young as well as the very old, have absolutely nowhere to turn for help with their special predicaments. Many of them gravitate to the areas where tourists gather in hopes of begging for some money. The children seem to have an advantage in collecting money from the tourists, and therefore are pushed hard to cash in on their advantage. They are relentless and fight hard to get the attention of any tourist, at the same time fighting off the older boys who wait to take the money from them.

The fierce competition among these children causes them to crowd around customers, each child delivering a sales pitch that ranges from a simple question to a plea of sympathy for their survival. Some children have learned to be glib and engage tourists in conversation that will

Photo by Jim Dorsey

possibly earn them a big tip.

"Where are you from?", they will ask, hoping to engage visitors to their land, and if the answer is the USA, they will recite the capitols of each state correctly. It is a tribute both to their persistence and salesmanship that they have mastered sufficient vocabulary in several languages. If a visitor, in an effort to get rid of the seller, says that he will buy after a visit to the temples, it's a guarantee that no matter what exit is chosen, that child will be there to close the sale. It is clear that the sales made by these children are not for extra pocket money. For them it's a matter of necessity, all money going toward providing minimal survival for their family.

Adult amputees, mostly former Khmer soldiers, don't usually hang out at the temples but rather frequent the markets where they beg incessantly. They are often homeless and

The government gave a well-connected private company the concession to earn millions of dollars managing Cambodia's national symbol, Angkor Wat.

1920 Banteay Kdei East Gate

2008

jobless and can be recognized by the old military clothing and the Khmer hat now used to ask for donations. One of these soldiers, Touch Seourly, gathered some of these beggars from the marketplace and moved to a remote place away from Phnom Penh in order to create a village just for the amputees. Today the village is known as Vean Thom. There these men with no future or outside support clear the land, dig water wells, build shacks and farms, all in an attempt to be totally independent from the rest of the population.

Eventually other amputees would join this village, bringing their families and their slim hope for a better life, but mostly restoring some shred of dignity to these men. Despite an outside world that would turn away from these men, here in this village there was no stigma, even for

LANDMINES

those who spent their days begging. For those in this self-made village, life has some sense of normalcy, but for the approximately 45 thousand Cambodians who have lost their limbs to land mines, their lives are anything but normal.

For the few amputee musicians who situate themselves near the entrance of the temples, playing their traditional instrument, day in and day out, there is an unmistakable style that accompanies their music even if it is just for brief moments during their long days. As they provide sounds for the tourists from faraway places, they must feel that they are making a connection between the ancient Khmer culture and the condition of today's Khmer. They understand that by selling their CD's they are creating a permanent link to the temples that attract tourists from all corners of the globe. For the most part these

TOP LEFT PAGE: Child's drawing of a site before and after a landmine explosion
BOTTOM LEFT PAGE: Street vendors 1920
BOTTOM MIDDLE LEFT PAGE: Modern Cambodian Beer label
BOTTOM RIGHT LEFT PAGE: Village drawing by young boy

THIS PAGE
TOP LEFT: Musician with his prosthetic leg
TOP RIGHT: Street sweeper
BOTTOM: Prosthetic legs and shoes at temple entrance

photo by Bill Morse

In 2003, Colombia had the third-highest rate of land mine casualties in the world. The regions with the most land mine victims:

Afghanistan   847
Cambodia   772
Colombia   668

1920 Banteay Kdei Buddha in the Cella of the main Prasay

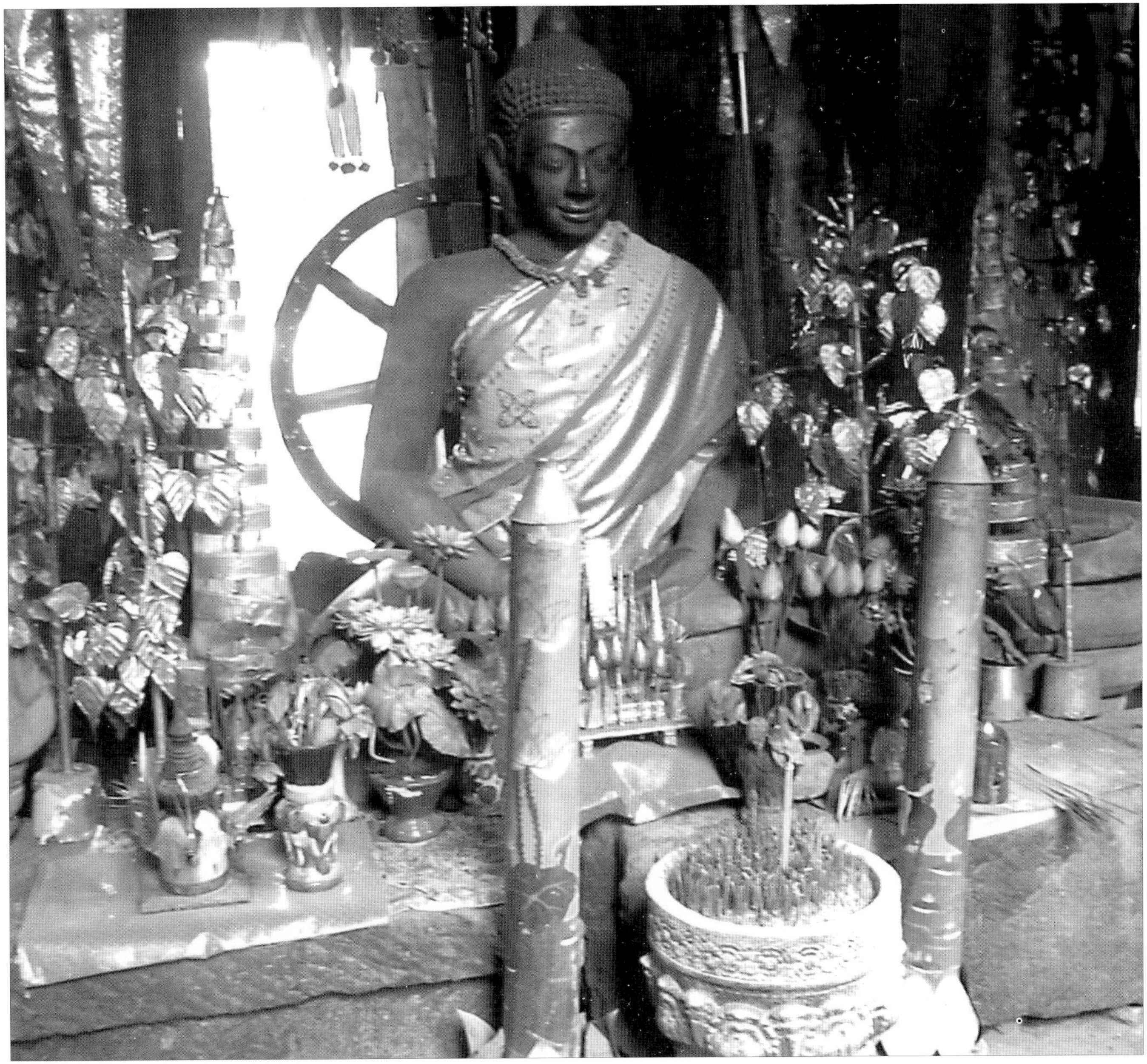

temples are all that remain of a proud culture.

It is clear that these monuments of this vanished culture are responsible for the emerging new Cambodian culture. Today's tourists allow a flicker of hope in keeping alive the spirit of the ancient great Khmer culture. The international companies and the government are, for the most part, not invested in the local population. The profit from exploiting all the national resources doesn't trickle down to the general population. Those who have not been allocated farmland are resigned each day to look down the road to see if the buses loaded with tourists have arrived at the gate of these temples. For them that is the only hope of having food for the family

Until recently visitors were advised to keep to all the clearly marked trails guiding them to all

TOP: Landmine museum display of deactivated mines
BOTTOM: Types of mines used in Cambodia

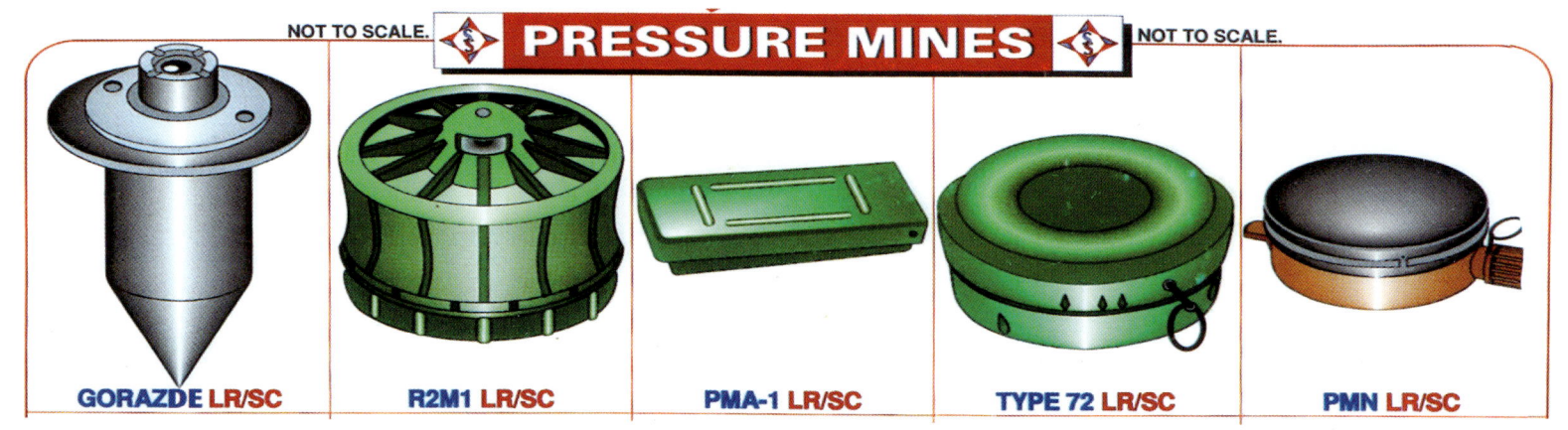

NOT TO SCALE. **PRESSURE MINES** NOT TO SCALE.

GORAZDE LR/SC — R2M1 LR/SC — PMA-1 LR/SC — TYPE 72 LR/SC — PMN LR/SC

the temples. Today most of the warnings at the most visited temples have been removed. The red danger signs with the skull and crossbones can still be seen and it is advised that one take this notice seriously. Side trips and individual explorations are not advised.

There would appear to be no real rush by anybody to clear these areas of the land mines or jungle overgrowth. There is so much to see and visit that it would take a tourist several days just to see all the safe areas that have been cleared. Even for the most seasoned tourist, what is accessible presents an overwhelming challenge. Physical limitations make it impossible to take in the full scope of Angkor Wat even for the most hale and hearty of tourists.

A two-day pass costs about $40, which only

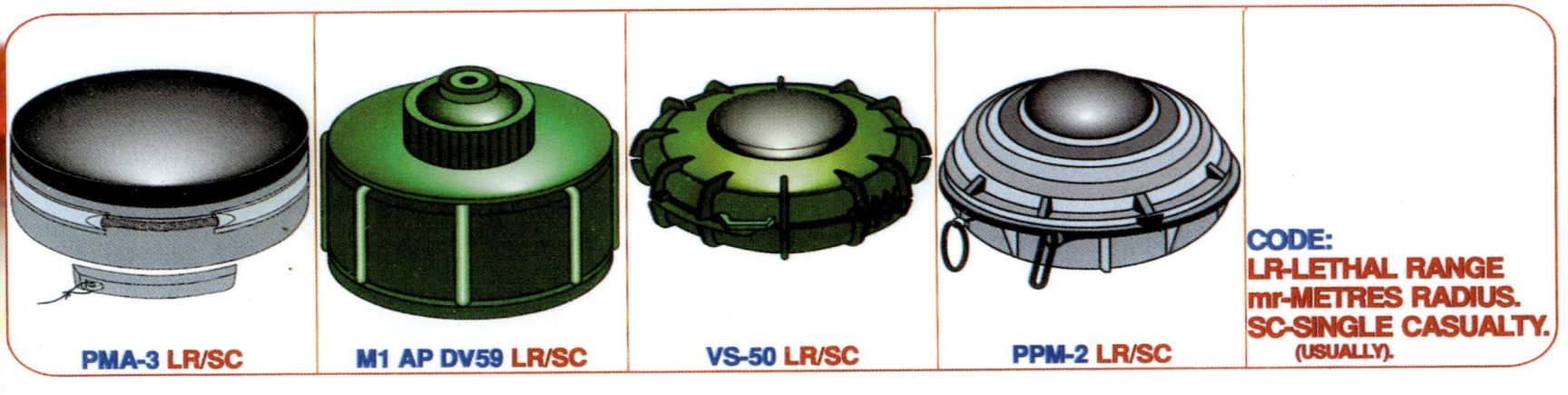

TOP: Landmine museum display
BOTTOM: Types of landmines used in Cambodia

PMA-3 LR/SC   M1 AP DV59 LR/SC   VS-50 LR/SC   PPM-2 LR/SC

CODE:
LR-LETHAL RANGE
mr-METRES RADIUS.
SC-SINGLE CASUALTY.
(USUALLY).

1920 Pre Rup AD 961 South corner Prasat

2009

THE KHMER ROUGE

Tuol Sleng Photo Archives

Tuol Sleng Photo Archives

TOP LEFT: Khmer Rouge soldiers in communal dinning area

TOP RIGHT: Khmer Rouge guards at Tuol Sleng Prison 1977

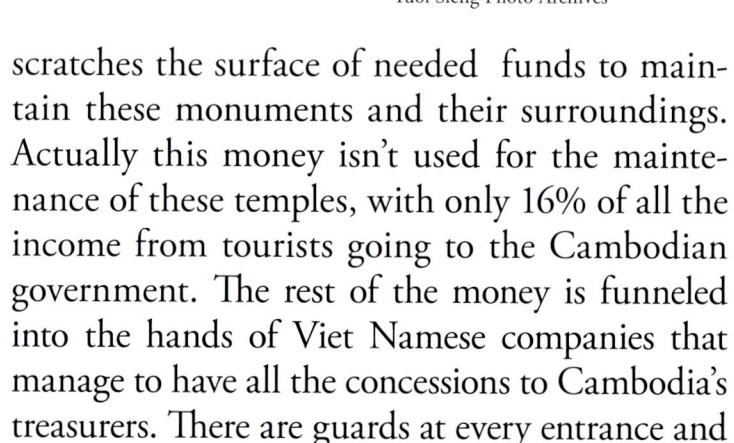

scratches the surface of needed funds to maintain these monuments and their surroundings. Actually this money isn't used for the maintenance of these temples, with only 16% of all the income from tourists going to the Cambodian government. The rest of the money is funneled into the hands of Viet Namese companies that manage to have all the concessions to Cambodia's treasurers. There are guards at every entrance and every exit to the temples checking passes at every turn and it is not clear who pays for these guards.

Special events with light and sound productions are staged periodically and they demand a steep entrance fee. As to where that profit is applied is anyone's guess, but when one sees scaffolding that has been in place on some parts of temples that have seen no workers on them for years, one wonders.

Scaffolding in use can be found in the eastern part of the Angkor Wat temple against the eastern gallery. This eastern gallery contains the most famous bas-relief in the temple. It is also

TOP LEFT: Khmer Rouge soldiers at Angkor Wat 1976

TOP RIGHT: Scaffolding used in restorations effort in 2009

Tuol Sleng Photo Archives

an important link to understanding the Khmer mythology. The 49-meter panel represents the conflict between the gods and the demons. The tug of war between these two forces is visualized through a very graphic depiction of giant Naga Vasohi, which is coiled around the image of mount Wandara. This conflict represents the churning of the cosmic sea and the universal search to find the sought-after elixir of immortality. This churning has been going on for thousands of years and in Khmer mythology it is believed that, before the world began, the gods were continually bothered by the demons and that is why they asked Vishnu to help relieve their torment. The answer was in finding the ambrosia that would guarantee immortality and it was to be found in the bottom of the ocean of milk. One of the most interesting aspects of this advice was that the gods would need to work together with the very demons they wanted to get rid of. The demons, for their involvement, were to be rewarded with some of the benefits of

1920 Wild Elephants in the Bayon Temple

2008

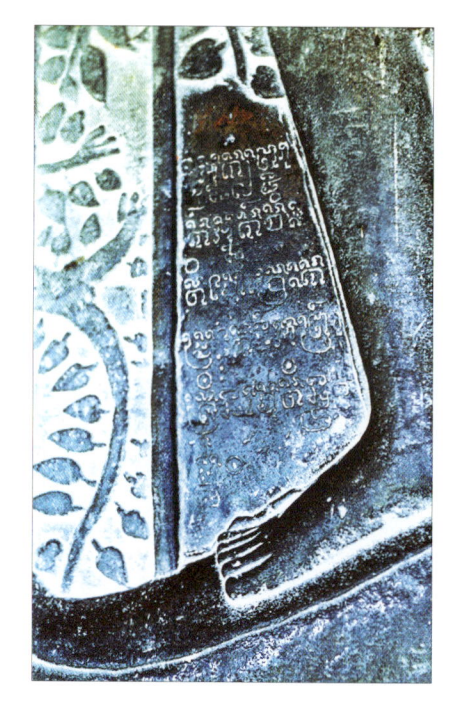

TOP LEFT: Khmer writing in Angkor Wat
TOP RIGHT: Bas relief of servants to the King
BOTTOM: Pigs transported to the market 2007

this highly coveted ambrosia.

In studying this 49-meter panel one can see the snake being pulled by two groups, the gods pulling the tail end and the demons the head of this snake. This act of churning the ocean of milk, as depicted in this panel, shows that the ambrosia was indeed found. During this churning process many more treasurers were found, including a three headed elephant, a moon god and the wonderful Apsaras.

The section of the eastern wall of this temple represents the core beliefs of the Khmer, defining the spirit and the essence of ancient Khmer culture . Today the workers climbing over theses scaffoldings are on a mission to preserve this panel from further damage caused by a leaky roof. The stains and deterioration of the actual stone is clearly visible and the need for action to prevent further damage is undeniable. Large panels have been put near the wall in order to explain to the visitor why this famous section is off limits to all tourists, some coming especially to view this part of Angkor Wat. Noted on these panels are several international organizations helping in this mission to save and restore these historic portrayals of Khmer history.

TOP LEFT: Foreign Warrior riding Elephant Bayon Bas Relief
TOP RIGHT: Replaced statue in hallway with modern umbrella

All structures at Angkor Wat, no mater how well engineered and constructed, when left to the elements of nature will eventually fall apart and vanish from sight. Constant maintenance is crucial to long range survival. Time is of the essence as is continual maintenance.

In the absence of a dedicated, concerted policy, there is instead one solitary soul who has dedicated his life to the continual maintenance of these ruins. Chhoun Keam at the Ta Prohm temple is hardly noticed by the swarm of visitors to that site. Each and every day he goes forth with his self-made broom and sweeps from one end to the other collecting the leaves that float to the floor of this temple . This task seems so futile and yet to him it is necessary and important.

Why did the massive urban complex at Angkor collapse in the 16th century? The First-ever complete, detailed map- made with NASA ground-sensing radar-provides fresh evidence that the city's residents may have overexploited their environment.

1920   Ta Prome Apsara celestial Dancers

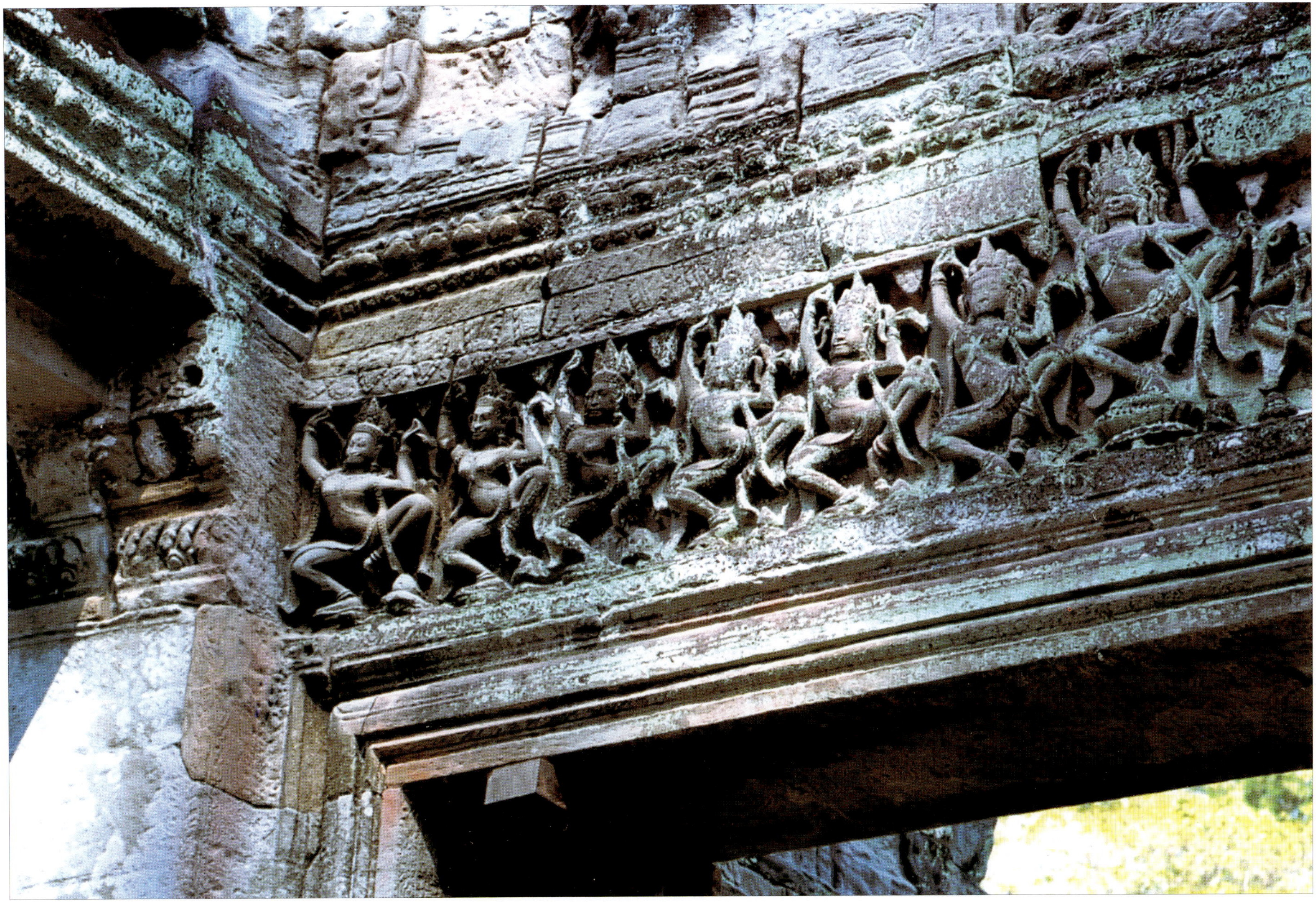

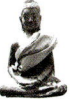

BOTTOM: Temple guard 1918, note crossbow
RIGHT: Chain and bathroom box at Tuol Sleng prison
FAR RIGHT: Photographs of killed citizens by the Khmer Rouge

In a plastic bag he collects the inevitable trash left by tourists carefully separating it from the leaves and twigs he gathers so gently. In observing Chhoun Keam during his endless carefully planned routine, it becomes very clear that there is much more to this lonely sweeper of the ruins. The tourists dropping their film cans and water bottles and candy wrappers on the floor could never imagine what that did to the heart and soul of this lone sweeper who takes his task so seriously.

He was a farmer living a marginal life tending to the livestock which he had done for most of his life. His story was not much different from all other Cambodians, but it took a turn when he encountered the French Archeologists and their discoveries of these ruins. He was so taken by these discoveries that he joined the field teams as a laborer hauling stones into their proper places. He was young and strong and his work and dedication was greatly needed. His life changed dramatically as it did for all Cambodians during

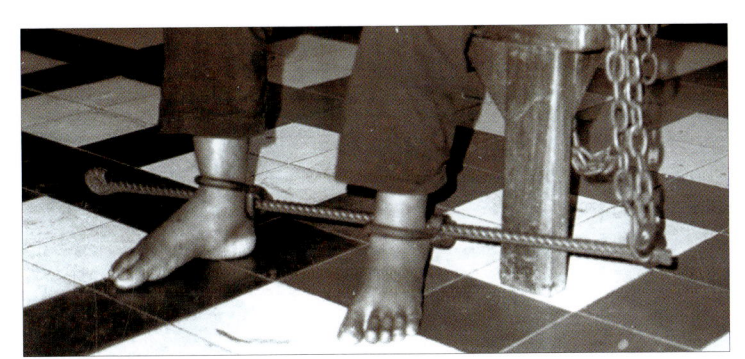

Tuol Sleng Photo Archives

Tuol Sleng Photo Archives

Tuol Sleng Photo Archives

Tuol Sleng Photo Archives

the 1970's when the Khmer Rouge took power, and proceeded with their brutal destruction, both of lives and property virtually destroying fabric of this ancient country. Despite the purging of nearly a million and a half Cambodians from the population, Chhoun Neam managed to survive. This man's most traumatic loss was when the Khmer came and took his two sons. Like so many of his countrymen, he believed that they would some day come home, but that never happened. Also like so many of his countrymen, it is reoccurring nightmare. To this day he dreams of their return, and carries a picture of him and his sons with him should they one day return to him. Today the picture is barely recognizable with faded images and worn edges, much like the fading of the temples he lovingly tends to each day.

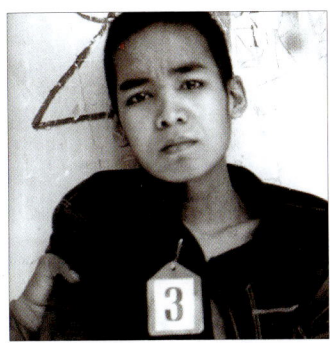

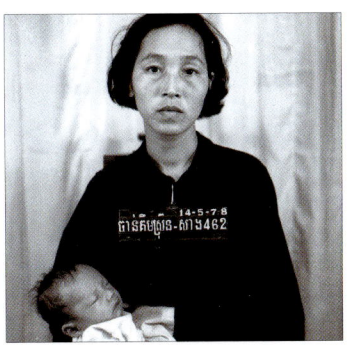

After the Khmer left in 1979 he could no longer help with the reconstruction efforts,

Mine clearance has frequently been linked to finding a needle in a haystack, but in Cambodia, finding the haystack was a problem in itself.

TOP LEFT: Leg irons used at Tuol Sleng prison
BOTTOM LEFT: Sculls excavated from mass grave
TOP MIDDLE: Photo ID of to be killed prisoners
FAR RIGHT: Photo enlarger and light stand used to Photograph Prisoners

1975   Tuol Sleng school house used as prison

KAING GUEK EAV the S-21 Tuol Sleng Prison Commandant known as Duch was sentenced to 35 years in prison on 26th July 2010 a term reduced to 19 years because of time served.

2009

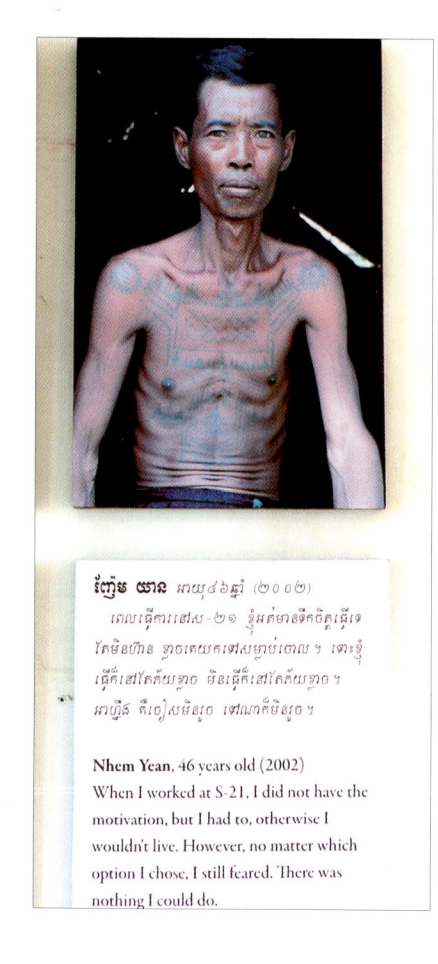

TOP LEFT: A survivors story displayed at Tuol Sleng Museum
TOP RIGHT: A young Cambodian girl reading the testimonies of survivors
BOTTOM: Shackle chains used by the Khmer Rouge

Nhem Yean, 46 years old (2002)
When I worked at S-21, I did not have the motivation, but I had to, otherwise I wouldn't live. However, no matter which option I chose, I still feared. There was nothing I could do.

but he could not stay away from these beloved monuments. He returned as a sweeper feeling he was still doing his part to for the survival of his Khmer cultural heritage. He sees that the temples again are under relentless attacks, by the weeds, vines and the steady stream of tourists. What little he can do, he does with a full heart and an abiding sense of honor.

Toward the end of his life this one man became something of an unofficial local attraction. It was indeed a sad day when the spot where he was reliably present was empty. The silence of his sweeping motions affected the small children that would gather around him on their break from selling post cards to the many visitors. These children listened so attentively to his stories and they were caught up in his devotion to this place and all that it meant to his people.

He was a silent inspiration for these kids most of whom were without parents of their own.

It was so touching in later years to see a small girl selling Chhoun's last elephant bells. She had known where he had hidden them in the ruins with all his meager belongings. Having been given a picture of the sweeper she was prompted to return the Gesture by handing over one of these elephant bells to a visitor who had come from a great distance to see this place. This bell today, so far from that unique origin, holds the spirit and the soul of a culture not yet lost.

This little girl in those ruins, holding several elephant bells for sale, carries forward a tenuous legacy. Will this child, and others like her, do what they can to protect and preserve a dying relic? The legacy of the temples is in the hands of a new generation. For the present there is the

Photo by Jim Dorsey

TOP LEFT: Author with Chhoun Keam in 2006

TOP RIGHT: Empty seat of Chhoun Keam 2008

1920   Apsara Dancers

2008

For the present there is the memory of an old sweeper and the example of one young girl ...

Pierre H Odier

Photo by Jim Dorsey

memory of an old sweeper and the example of one young girl selling bamboo elephant bells that connect a lost culture to an uncertain future for Cambodia.

TOP LEFT: Young girl selling Chhouns elephant bells after his death
TOP RIGHT: Author leaving Chhouns Keam's work spot
BOTTOM: One of Chhouns elephant bells

126

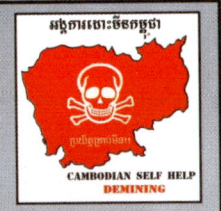

CAMBODIAN DEMINING

"My only goal in life is to make my country safe for my people" Aki Ra

Amongst the various national and international organizations that make an effort to clear Cambodia of land mines there's one heroic, social conscious man, whose name is Aki Ra. Since the end of the 30 year war he has made it his personal mission to clear the mine fields of his country.

As was the fate of many orphans, Aki Ra fell into the hands of the Khmer Rouge forces who trained him to become a child soldier, after they killed his parents. Children like Aki Ra were frequently used to find the disarm land mines in enemy territory. Their small fingers were considered ideal for the delicate task of unscrewing fuses of the mines. If a child made a mistake there many more orphans to fill the sudden vacancy.

Aki Ra made no mistakes, and with additional de-mining training, he's now considered one of the world's foremost de-mining experts. Since the end of the conflict he has cleared the vegetation of overgrown mine fields with machetes and probed the earth with sticks, uncovering and disarming over 50,000 land mines. Presently he employs some thirty men whom he has trained to help him with his dangerous task. Ake Ra recently acquired two used metal detectors from proceeds of donations to the non-profit fund raising organization, the Cambodia Land Mine Museum & Relief Facility which he founded.

The non-governmental organization, CLMMRF, currently houses 30 youngsters who have been injured by land mines. Because these children can neither work on the family farms nor walk the often long distances to schools, Aki Ra offered to accommodate them at his museum compound. There the children are educated and trained in skills other than farming and manual labour. Unlike many land mine victims, who turn to begging as a means of survival, the children and youths who are cared for by Aki Ra and his wife Hourt are able to live with dignity and hope.

Ten years ago Canada initiated an international movement to stop the manufacture, trade and use of land mines; 122 nations sent representatives to Ottawa to sign a treaty to implement this agreement. It included a committed effort to clear the world's mine fields.

LEFT: Cambodian self help Demining brochure
ABOVE: Aki Ra seen in the field

Aki Ra's Demining team in the field Demining farm land

CAMBODIAN SELF HELP
DEMINING

All the proceeds (profits) from this publication will go to support the mine clearing efforts of Cambodian Self Help Demining and the children who live at the Cambodia Landmine Museum Childrens' Center

Displays at the Landmine museum and the children living at the museum

129

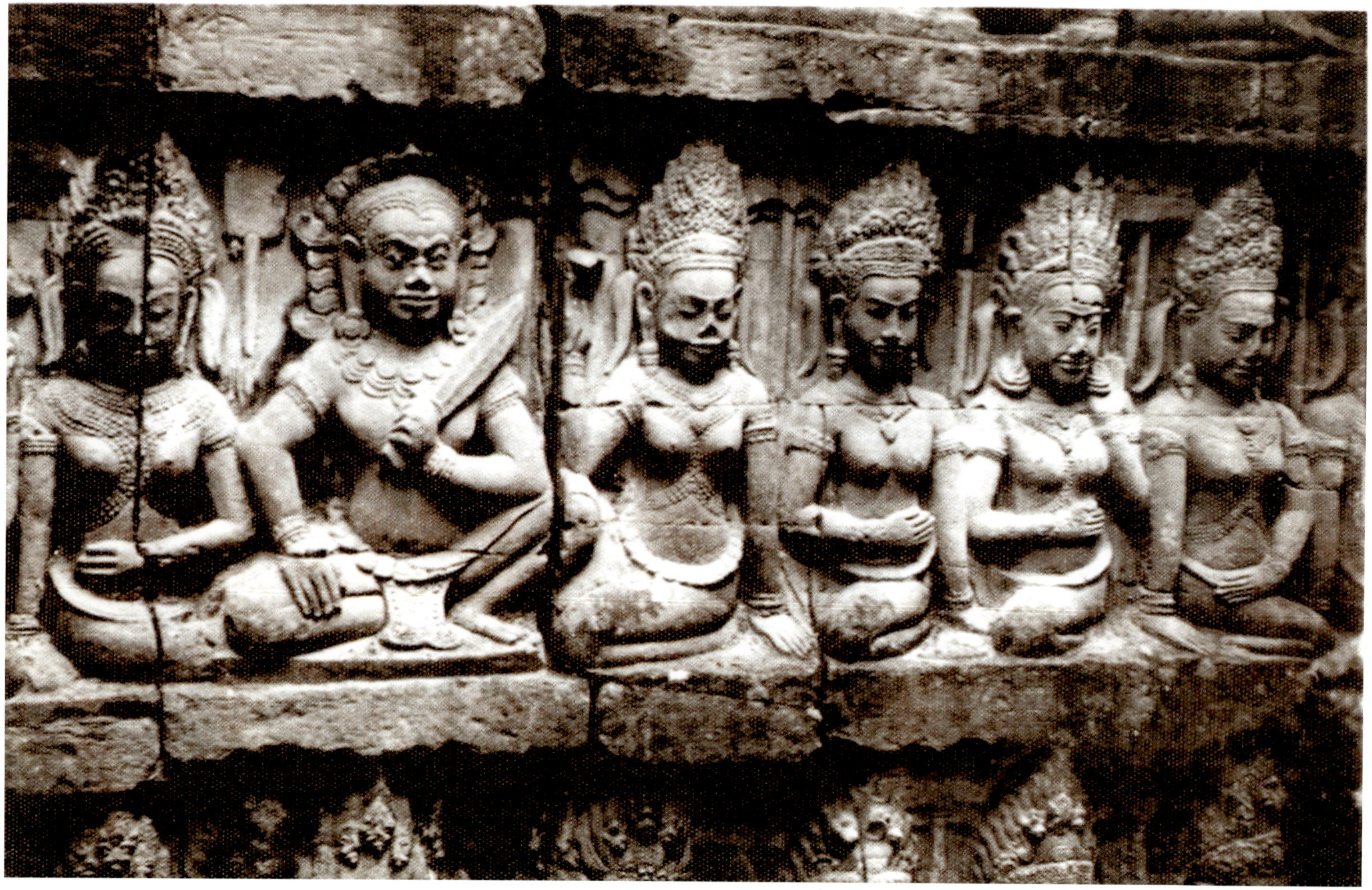

POSTSCRIPT

What then is the future for Cambodia?

Today half of the Cambodian population is under 20 and 80% of the total population is lives in rural villages struggling to eke out a minimal existence. An elder generation that has managed to survive the atrocities of the past is too exhausted to confront its trauma. For the younger generation it is hard to believe that it is possible that such brutality could have been done to Cambodians by Cambodians. The prime Minister of the royal government Hun Sen sums up the mood of a nation in saying to his people, "Dig a hole and bury the past."

Perhaps in the grand scheme of things there is wisdom and healing that comes from forgiving and forgetting, but there is a well known adage as well that tells us that, "Those who do not remember the past are condemned to repeat it." The future of the Cambodian people may well depend on their willingness to find a balance between the two.

BIBLIOGRAPHY

ALBANESE MARILIA. The Treasures of Angkor. White Star Publishing Vercelli Italy, 2006.
BRIGGS LAWRENCE PALMER. The Ancient Khmer Empire. Philadelphia U.S.A., 1951.
CASEY ROBERT. Four Faces of Siva. The Bobbs Merrill Comp. New York U.S.A., 1929
CHANDLER DAVID P. The Tragedy of Cambodian History. Yale Press NewYork.1991.
    "   "   A history of Cambodia. Yale Press New York. 1992.
CLARK A HEATHER. When there was no Money. Springer Heidelberg Germany. 2006.
CLAYES JEAN YVES. Angkor. Boy-Landry Phnom Penh Cambodia 1949.
COUGILL WYNNE. Stilled Lives. Documentation Center of Cambodia Phnom Penh, Cambodia 2004
CROLL MIKE. The history of Landmines. Pen & Swords Book LTD. Barnsley, Great Britain 1998.
DE BEERKSI JEANNERAT P. Angkor Ruins in Cambodia. Houghton Mifflin Comp. Boston U.S.A. 1924.
DY KHAMBOLY. A History of Democratic Kampuchea. Documentation Center Of Cambodia. Phnom Penh 2007.
FREEMAN MICHAEL. Ancient Angkor. Weatherhill Ct.06611 U.S.A. 1999.
    "   "   A Golden Souvenir of Angkor. Pacific Rim Press. Hong Kong 1992.
HARRIS LORD. A Visit to Angkor Wat 1882. Wordman Books. Maryland U.S.A. 2002.
HEYWOOD DENISE. Cambodian Dance(Celebration of the Gods). River Books. Bangkok Thailand 2008.
HIGHAM CHARLES. The Civilization of Angkor. Butler& Tanner LTD. London 2001.
HUMAN RIGHTS WATCH. Landmines in Cambodia. Asia Watch U.S.A. 1991.
ISHIZAWA YOSHIAKI. Along the Royal Roads to Angkor. Weatherhill New York 1999.
JACQUES CLAUDE. Angkor. Koeneman Verlagsgesellschaft Cologne Germany 1999.
JESSUP HELEN IBBITSON. Art & Architecture of Cambodia. Thames & Hudson. London U.K. 2004.
KIERNAN BEN. The Pol Pot Regime. Silkworm Books Chiang Mai Thailand 1997.
LAUR JEAN. Angkor an illustrated Guide to the Monuments. Flammarion Paris France. 2002.

MACDONALD MALCOLM. Angkor and the Khmers. Oxford University Press. London. 1987.
MAGUIRE PETER. Facing Death in Cambodia. Columbia University Press. New York. 2005.
MEMOIRES ARCHEOLOGIQUES Tom II. Le Temple D'Angkor Vat
          (La Galerrie des Bas Reliefs)
          Les Editions G. Van Oest. Paris France 1932.
    "   "   " Le Temples D'Angkor Vat.
          (La Sculpture Ornemental du Temple)
          Les Edition G. Van Oest. Paris France 1930.
    "   "   " Le Temples D'Angkor Vat.
          (L'Architecture du Monument)
          Les Edition G. Van Oest. Paris France 1929.
NADAL. Ruins D'Angkor. Braun & Cie. Dorwach France 1921.
NARUM KEO. Apsara Dance .The ministry of Culture. Phnom Penh Cambodia 2003.
NGOR HAINE. Surviving the Killing Fields. Chatto Winrus. London 1988.
PONCHAUD FRANCOIS. Cambodia Year Zero. Holt Rinehart. New York 1977.
PRAN DITH. Children of Cambodia's Killing Fields. Silkworm Books Chiang Mai. Thailand 1997.
RAWSON PHILIP. The Art of Southeast Asia. Thames & Hudson New York 1967.
ROONEY DAWN. Angkor. Odyssey Publication LTD. Hong Kong. 1999.
Shawcross William. The Qualaty of Mercy. Simon & Schuster. New York U.S.A., 1984.
SHORT PHILIP. Pol Pot: Anatomy of a Nighmare. Henry Holt & Company. New York. 2004.
SNELLGROVE DAVID. Angkor Before and After. Weatherhill. INC. CT. 06611. U.S.A. 2004.
STIERLIN HENRI. Angkor and Khmer Art. Agence Internationale Paudex Switzerland. 1997.
STONE RICHARD. Divining Angkor. National Geographic Washington U.S.A. 2009.
UNG LOUNG. First they Killed my Father. Harper& Collins. New York U.S.A. 2000.
VECCHIA STEFANO. The Khmers. White Star Publishing Vercelli Italy 2007.
VICKERY MICHAEL. Cambodia 1975-1982. Silkworm Books Chiang Mai Thailand, 1999.
YATHAY PIN. Stay Alive my Son. Silkworm Books Chiang Mai Thailand, 2000.